Life on High Alert

HANNAH RAINEY

ACKNOWLEDGMENTS

This book simply wouldn't have been possible without the support and advice from those around me - this has been a difficult experience. Thanks to those who have given both advice and time to helping me get a young girl's story heard and turning a dream into a very real experience.

Special thanks to my Dad and Beth for providing some not-so-nice details and helping me to piece together some events that I had little memory or knowledge of for the purpose of this book – I hope it was worth the wait.

Thanks to Charlie for your endless support throughout this process and always.

And finally, to four-year-old me: this is for you.

ONE

It snowed the day I was born. The South East London sky – so often grey and drab – was full of crisp, white snowflakes. A nice addition to the occasion: the young newlywed couple in the snow, taking their new-born home. Sweet. My dad cried when I was born.

Mum and dad were young – just a little younger than I am now – I think it's quite unbelievable: the thought of having a child now makes me feel a bit unwell. They'd married the month before I was born, my mother popping out of her two-piece.

I can imagine my dad carrying me in a car seat, my mum following on, looking at us, full of joy as her husband carried their brand new, perfect baby girl home.

I was two when my parents split and filed for divorce. I have no recollection of it. They'd been together around seven years and together since their teens – but now it had all come to a life-shattering halt. I lived with my mum and saw my dad on weekends. There was probably no dispute over it – it was just what was done. I don't imagine her telling my dad that I absolutely had to go with her and I don't imagine there being much question about it: where mums went, children went.

Eventually, both my parents met somebody new. My dad's new girlfriend, Beth, worked in my Dad's local pub whilst studying a Psychology degree at Greenwich University. She was welcoming and made an effort to get along with me.

My mum's new boyfriend, James*, was quite different. Very different from my dad – I will never understand how she went from one to the other. My dad is very stubborn but gentle really, and he would never, ever hurt me in any way. James was different. I don't know where they met, or how she came across somebody like him. A criminal: drugs, anti-social behaviour, assault; he had a long list of proud achievements – and he really was smugly proud of them. He was insufferable: manipulative, arrogant, immoral.

I remember his face vaguely; tanned skin and brown hair with dark eyes, but not much else. But I remember his presence with a genuine sense of unease.

My life was about to change, but of course I had no idea how my future, life and personality would be so drastically altered from that point. It's frustrating to give this man so much power, and to acknowledge that his actions would change my life forever but unfortunately, that's exactly what he did.

To me his behaviour was frankly disgusting, in a way that is hard to comprehend or articulate. He was proudly insolent and very willing to exert his authority – even though he didn't need to. He enjoyed making people feel terrified of him, and it worked. He'd get desperately violent, as if something inside him took over any sense of self-control, and he became vicious, unforgiving, and passionately destructive.

He fed a puppy marijuana and killed it. Sometimes, when he came home, he'd throw things across a room. It was like he was reminding himself – and us – of his own power; a belligerent 'I'm back.' I'd hide away and listen to our things shatter as they fell, but his ability to damage people emotionally was just as strong as it was physically. I guess he made my mother believe that she'd never find anybody else, and that she couldn't live without him, so she'd better just get on with it. I've tried to understand that power dynamic, but I've never been able to grasp the concept of physically and willingly hurting another person just because you feel like it.

It wasn't just me who was mistreated. He hurt my mother, but I don't remember it all that well. I have wondered whether, sometimes, she took it so that I didn't have to, or whether she just accepted that both her and I would be tortured often and that, well, that was the life we had. I don't know if she ever tried to leave.

I saw her scolded with boiling juice; heard her scream as the liquid burned her. In fact, it's sounds that have stayed with me more than anything else. My mum crying, myself crying, my own breath as I tried to catch it, things shattering. And silence: silence could be the most powerful sound of all.

I knew silence as two things: it was the sound of the aftermath; the sound of having nothing left; absolutely nothing more to give. And it was the sound of hiding. Finding a little cupboard and squeezing into it, or another small space that would conceal me for a little while, covering my mouth so that nobody could hear me breathing, trying desperately not to cough or sneeze and betray my hiding place. Squeezing my eyes shut and hoping that I wouldn't be found.

But you're always found.

Dog leads became whips and hands became fists. He'd pinch my ears and drag me from room to room, burn my skin with cigarettes or marijuana joints, and spit in my face. He'd hold my head under the water in the bath, sink or toilet. Paralysis: fear would overtake my body like nothing I'd ever known before. Everything hurt, emotionally and physically, but the dunking made me feel like I might die. The thought of it now makes me struggle for breath – the feeling of just being unable to catch any oxygen and longing to fill your lungs before dizziness sets in, but you can't give up - if you do, you'll drown.

I can imagine myself coughing as he releases his grip, gasping for breath, and forcing air back into my lungs but, truthfully, I don't remember what happened afterwards. I don't remember anything he said to me, or how I felt coming out of the water, or what I did after. I just remember the feeling of a grip on the back of my head, my hair, and just trying to hold my breath for as long as I could.

I wasn't allowed to speak much and if I spoke when I shouldn't, James would take out thick grey tape and cover my mouth with it. The sight and sound

8

of it made my stomach churn: I was helpless.

I had two things for comfort: the first, a dog toy my dad had given me. I named it Freddie, and it accompanied me everywhere. The second, a pet fish. I don't remember when or where we got it or how that came about and now, the only real memory I have of that fish is James taking it out of its tank, and then hacking into it with red scissors – children's ones - cutting it into small pieces right before my eyes.

I wasn't a naughty child – I couldn't be – but somehow whatever I did, it was always out of line. I was clearly an unwanted presence – and he made damn sure I knew it. He wanted my Mother to himself.

Would it all be easier to deal with now, if I'd been able to remember what my mother had said or done? If I knew she had tried to help me? If I could remember her exchanging glances with me across the room, with eyes that said 'it'll be alright, babe'? I guess I'll never know.

I don't remember what my relationship with my mother was like back then; the memories are lost. I just remember him: his drug-fueled eyes and lips that spat venom. I remember big bruises on a tiny body.

He must've been smart. They both were - I looked well cared for. My body was always covered – I was an immaculately dressed child - and every hair would always be in place. Perfectly blow-dried straight, despite my natural curls.

Obviously he knew what he was doing physically, he knew how to get away with it, and he knew how to get my mother on his side. He knew how to make her believe that he wouldn't touch again – until a couple of days later, when I'd hear the grey tape being ripped from the roll, or the sound of the bath running would put stone cold fear into my body.

Whether she genuinely believed that he treated us right, or she turned a blind eye to it, I think she must have loved him. Or was she just terrified? Like I was. Maybe it was a mixture of both. Maybe she thought he would kill us.

Now, as an adult, I find myself wondering what I would have done if I had been the one in mum's situation with an abuser. Would I have fled, leaving him and his lifestyle behind, without ever looking back? Or would I have stayed, in the hope that somehow, he would change. Perhaps even thinking that I could have made him change if he really loved me, for you don't deliberately hurt the people that you love.

Maybe I'd have been too terrified to leave. Maybe he'd have come after us anyway. Maybe he really would have been able to manipulate me, to make me truly believe that the life I had with him was the best I could get. But what would I have done for my daughter? I do believe that you don't know what you would do in this kind of situation until you find yourself in it, but I hope that I would have scooped up my child and run for our lives without looking back. I don't know, and I hope that I never have to find out.

Although I think he was smart for manipulating my mum, he was pretty bloody stupid to be caught out the way he was. Really it was quite foolish for him, but very lucky for my mum and me.

I don't know what day it was, what time it was, in fact I don't remember a single moment of it. But as a result of his previous activities he already had a probation officer, and he was expected to report to him regularly so that the probation service could keep tabs on him. But he hadn't been checking in. Who knows why. Maybe it was his arrogance. Maybe he thought he could get away with anything – until the day his probation officer stopped by our house. My mother had a big bump on her head, and my face was purple from the eyes down.

I wish I could remember it: the moment of release. I don't know if I understood this at the time. I don't know if I understood the severity of the situation – probably not, I was still only four – or how my life would now change again. I wish I could remember the probation officer's face, he was the man who saved me from a potentially life-threatening situation, and yet I have nothing to do with him now. I know nothing of him.

I was rarely seen by any other people during my time with my mum and James. I barely saw my dad. They must have been too scared of him seeing the signs. If I had any visible injuries, I would be made to tell him that I'd fallen off my bike, walked into something, or fallen over. When it got worse, they'd make up some excuse – one week I was too ill to visit; the next I was busy doing something else. Sometimes, they would tell him I didn't want to go. It breaks my heart to know that now.

I barely left the house. I wasn't allowed to go to nursery – someone would have noticed the bruises. Then finally, that one day, somebody did notice. And suddenly, it was all out of her control.

I was taken to hospital to have my injuries checked out, and stayed there for a night, by myself. Nobody else was allowed to see me. Not mum, not dad, not a family friend. It was as if I was in quarantine. The authorities had to find out what had happened before either parent could get anywhere near me, so I was left in the company of medical and legal professionals.

I can remember my body being checked by a doctor, who I see in my mind as being much, much bigger than me. She was looking over me, looking at every single part of my body.

My face was marked yellow and blue from the eyes down. There were more than thirty bruises of differing ages disguising the skin from my eyes down to my knees, my body decorated with a multitude of various colours. Malnourished and dehydrated, my skin was dry and grey all over apart from the blue, yellow, brown, purple splodges. I felt cold and wished I had a jumper. My bare arms were available for all to see, coloured splodges on display. Usually they'd be hidden.

Finally my Dad was allowed in to see me, but I don't remember that moment. I don't know if that's good or bad. I find it upsetting to think of my Dad getting a call to say that his four-year-old daughter is in hospital but he's not allowed anywhere near her. Shortly I was taken to the police station – I don't remember what happened here, but it was decided that I wouldn't be allowed to live with my mother anymore.

So I went home with my dad, and we both tried to start again.

TWO

I was taken to the flat my Dad shared with Beth late at night with a Child Protection Officer - later my mother would drop off some more of my belongings. I don't know when that happened – when she was allowed to see me, whether she was investigated in any way, or what happened to her. I don't remember seeing her.

In the flat I was given my own room, which we filled with things that I liked. Beth and my Dad thought it would be a good idea to get me two fish and a tank to put them in - I didn't tell them about what had happened to the last one I had. Maybe they knew.

But even though I had this new life, it took time to adjust to the way that I was living. It was so different to the life I'd lived so far. When I first arrived at the flat I would wait outside the living room when my parents were in it, because I thought I wasn't allowed to go in. I was used to hovering outside of rooms, always waiting to be spoken to – that was the way I had been taught to behave. Whenever they saw me doing this, they would tell me to join them and I would go and sit on the floor. I'd learned that I was too naughty to sit on the sofa: only adults could do that. Children had to sit on the floor and daren't even think that they were good enough for a seat.

It took some time for me to believe what my Dad and Beth told me; to understand that I was not necessarily a bad child. Not only could I sit on the sofa if I wanted to, but it turned out that that was actually the normal thing to do.

My understanding of normal life, and healthy family life, was incredibly warped.

I can understand how this would be just as difficult for my Dad and Beth as it was for me. This child has come into their home with a complete misunderstanding of life, and I guess parenting is hard enough as it is. I can imagine that I was a difficult child to parent at this stage.

I had become timid and clingy. Before the move, I used to stick to my mother's side as closely as I could. I wouldn't play with anything. Was that because I didn't know if that was allowed, and was worried it would get me into trouble? Or was it because I hadn't even learned how to play happily? I don't know.

Beth and Dad taught me how to be a child. They taught me that it was okay to want to play with a toy, or even to go and play with other children, if that was what I wanted. The longer I lived with them, the more my confidence grew, and my relationship with Beth strengthened. She took to the role of being a mum quickly - despite it probably not being what she'd signed up for - and began to show me how it really should be.

I don't know if she'd known about me from the start of her relationship with my Dad, but I am sure that it wouldn't have occurred to her that she'd become my Mother full time. I think it's a strange and difficult situation to willingly put yourself into, but she did.

She bought me new clothes, played with me, taught me. I wasn't used to any of that. She washed my clothes, cooked for me, and made sure I ate my breakfast, and took my vitamins before school. She made sure I ate my vegetables, but she bought me lots of the foods that I really liked too. She was the one who was there for me when I had tonsillitis and chicken pox at the same time. We listened to boybands, watched films, and I was often either reading stories or writing them.

Most of all, I was treated like a little girl. It turned out that, whilst living in the flat, my fish – Phil and Grant – died multiple times. I was none the wiser. I just thought they were the same old fish – really hardy, long-lasting fish! I suppose I never thought about it at that age. But really my parents were secretly replacing them with new goldfish each and every time one passed, just so that I wouldn't know. Eventually there came a time – when my parents had probably spent quite enough money on goldfish, and I was stronger emotionally – when they told me that my (last) pair of fish had died, and we consigned them to a watery grave in the time-honoured tradition of flushing them down the loo.

Beth gave me all the things I had been missing before. She gave me the "Mum" things, all the stuff that I saw in films and on TV, read in books, and heard other people talking about. She cared for me the way a mum was supposed to, and she let me have my freedom too. No longer did I have to worry about going into a room I wasn't supposed to, or doing something that deep-down I knew wasn't bad, but would still have got me into trouble at my mum's house. There were no dog leads, no kicking or punching, no hands reaching for the back of my neck to push me under water.

But there was one thing that I still had from my past life. One link to that part of my life that I couldn't let go of quite so easily: my mother.

I saw her on weekends at first, but only if there was someone else there, usually my dad, Beth, or my maternal grandfather. We would have to be in an environment that was safe, something that had been checked out before, or at my dad's house. It took a while before she was allowed to take me to her own flat or her sister's house. My grandfather was often with us at this time – he would pick me up from school with my mum and drive us somewhere in town or take us back home to my Dad.

I was always happy to have my Grandad with us. He was soft and gentle, and he thought I was the best thing since sliced bread, so I'm told. I was the first grandchild on my mother's side of the family, and we became very close. He was a warm person who always had time for me, and I loved spending time with him. There are photos of us – me as a baby – and him looking down at me with loving eyes. I remember him well: dark grey hair, glasses, and he always seemed to have tanned skin, as if he'd just returned from a holiday.

It's fair to say that I was unsure of my Mother for a while on those weekend visits, but having my Grandad there gave it an element of safety: I always felt he was trustworthy, loving. He was gentle.

I don't think he knew what was happening to my Mum and me, and I wonder if she ever turned to him for support. I don't know the answer, but I know that he would have been there for her, if she'd tried. I can't imagine not ever turning to anyone in a situation like that, but I guess you don't know how you'd behave in these situations until you're in them.

He came to court with us too. There were two court cases over a number of years: one to establish contact arrangements between my mum and me, and another in which my mum and her boyfriend would be questioned, scrutinised and eventually sentenced. The ins and outs of my childhood were unpicked gradually, photos from my time at the hospital were shown and given as evidence.

My nursey teacher – who I had seen sporadically – gave evidence, too. My mother claimed that some injuries had been formed during my time at nursery, implying that it was their responsibility, not hers. It would have made things so much easier for her if it'd been shown that I'd been falling off of things, knocking my head, the usual. But my teacher informed the court that my name had never once appeared in the accident book.

I had to give evidence too. Barristers asked questions via video link, and I had to try and answer them as much as I could. I was four years old. I had no idea of the seriousness of what was happening. I had no idea what a court really was, what my parents were getting up to in there, or why we were there in the first place. I sat in front of a large screen, in which I could see an arrangement of people in what appeared to be dresses – I'd never seen a man in a dress before. Apparently, the barristers removed their wigs so that I wouldn't be scared.

I was happy to sit and answer what was asked – I had a friendly lady with me who provided teddy bears that would help me explain and demonstrate things that had happened. I sat in a plastic chair, swinging my legs innocently, showing the court room how things had been, with innocent teddy bear actors for reference.

It was an intense and aggressive case. James kept shouting things across the room; he said that my dad should have raised me better, that I was a bad child, and that none of this would have happened if I wasn't such a nightmare.

At the end of it, my mother was charged with neglect, and James with ABH (Actual Bodily Harm) and neglect. He was given a two-year suspended sentence. That meant he was able to walk out of court relatively freely and go on living his life – with my mother or not. I assume he had to report to another probation officer, although if his previous attitude was anything to go by, he probably wouldn't.

My mother also avoided a prison sentence by revealing that she was pregnant - something that nobody had known about until then. As a child I didn't know much of this – I had little understanding of what was really happening or the fact that actually both James and my Mum had managed to get off pretty lightly. It's only as an adult now that I can and have formed my own opinion, and quite frankly I don't think that justice was served at all. He will walk the streets, day after day, and probably corrupt other lives. Maybe he'll rip other children from their mothers, maybe he'll even take it too far for one family. What if he hits another child too hard? What if he actually drowns someone else?

Now, my Mother will never be free. With a child together, she will be tied to him always.

It was a long process, and while it was happening, we moved to Kent. Beth's family lived there, and I didn't mind too much about moving. I was too young to have any investment in the place I was leaving.

Before we made the move to Kent, we had a

barbecue on the rooftop of the flat, where I met all of Beth's family: her mum, her brothers, and some family friends. We ate burgers and sausages, and despite my tendency to be timid and withdrawn, I enjoyed myself. I was starting to learn that the world wasn't filled with violence. I didn't see anyone shout at each other, didn't see any plates get smashed, and I didn't see anyone get hurt.

We moved in with Beth's mum who was a widow now living on her own, and stayed there until we found a house we wanted. Her home was big and fun. There were toys everywhere, hundreds of books, a cupboard full of pens and paper for whenever I wanted them. The garden was huge, with concrete circling the lawn, which meant I could ride my scooter around and around for as long as I liked.

The first Christmas I can remember was at that house. I was about four, and I'd woken up excruciatingly early having been made aware of the prospect of Father Christmas – and he didn't disappoint. I opened my eyes at the crack of dawn to the sight of a room overflowing with gifts; parcels of all different shapes and sizes spilling into the hallway.

THREE

Beth's mum, who I call my Nan, became an intrinsically important part of my childhood. She was always kind, funny, safe.

She was the one who taught me how to swim. When we moved in to her house, I was terrified of water and would never want to get in it. When I had to wash my hair after swimming, I wouldn't put my head completely under the water in the shower. I would stand with one foot in the water and one foot out of it, and I remember our conversations about how I couldn't wash my hair without getting it wet. She tells me how, when we first started going to the pool, I would cling to my dad and scream if anybody came near me. Eventually my Dad didn't need to come anymore and we went by ourselves every week – I eventually gained a bit more confidence and started to learn proper lessons with other children. We always got chips and ice cream afterwards.

When I was nineteen, she took me on a cruise in Egypt, just the two of us, along the River Nile. We climbed obelisks, visited temples, snorkeled in the water. The ocean was rough and I'm still a bit wary of open water even now, but when I'm with her, I just feel like I can do it. We visited Cairo for the day, a scarily busy city. It reminded me of London but busier and boiling, with people running everywhere, shouting, car horns in the air. I felt like I was a sardine in a tin, people brushing past me as they hurried off to do whatever they needed. But my Nan has been safe from the start. She was never, at any point, even questionable to my young and disrupted mind.

After living with her for a while, my parents found a house just around the corner from her that we moved into. It was much bigger than the flat and I had the top floor to myself: my bedroom and my playroom.

I started a new school in Kent, in Year One, after completing my first year of school whilst we were still in London. When I started at this new school, I was carefully watched for some time by teachers who had to report back on me and my behaviour. My progress was pretty good at school and I enjoyed it, and I'm sure this was helped hugely by the lovely teacher I had in my first year. She was very gentle, a calming, stable influence, and I think she just genuinely really cared about us all. A classic, stereotypical primary school teacher. She produced reports and sent letters home to my dad, updating him about how I was doing in school. She knew about everything and had to keep an eye on me.

I made a best friend in school pretty quickly. We were in the same class throughout the whole of primary school and sat with each other, ate lunch together, played games together. We were constantly told off for chatting. I went over to her house all the time, playing with her two little sausage dogs who I thought were just the cutest things ever. We made milkshakes and ate pizza and stayed up late talking about silly things.

We were so inseparable that I knew her mother better than my own biological one. I didn't think anything about this at the time, I was most likely too young to realise the absurdity of it all, but now looking back, I realise just how strange it really is. Though I had started to accept that my stepmother was acting as my mother, I couldn't just pretend that I didn't have another - that I didn't have a biological one. It was always in the back of my mind that I was the child with two mums.

I was still seeing her, my biological mum, on weekends throughout my first few years of school. The three of us, me, my dad, Beth, all had mixed emotions about it. Beth later told me that she felt nervous about it every time I left. It was scary for us all, because we never knew if James was going to be there, or if he knew, or if he was around. My mother had had her second child, a boy, by this point and she would bring him along on her visits.

The two of them would come to the house with my grandfather and pick me up to go to the park or into town, but nowhere else. The court had allowed her to take me to a place and had decided when and for how long, and there was nothing to be done about that. But even though the court had drawn up particular rules about how she should conduct herself, she would still do things that weren't allowed. Like drive without a licence, or take me out of the area they had sectioned for us, or even see her ex, which was something she definitely was told not to do. She had sworn in court that she would stay away from him, that she had put an end to their relationship, so that it would be safe for me to see her. But, unfortunately, it was just one of many promises she didn't keep. All of this meant that every time I knew I had to go and see her, I would become agitated. I just didn't know that I could trust her. I didn't want to be around her because of all that had happened, and I had built a new life in Kent - but she was my Mother. I felt constantly torn.

After a while, I began making excuses to not see her. She wrote to me on colourful paper and enclosed stamped envelopes so that I could reply if I wanted, but I didn't. She called sometimes, not always when she said she would, but I often gave short answers. She often asked the same questions – about school, about swimming, about ballet lessons – and I didn't know what to say to her. They were brief conversations. Awkward, even. She'd tell me that when she next saw me we'd be going swimming, or perhaps to the park, but it didn't often happen. When I look back now I think it's probably for the best that we didn't go swimming together - and I wonder if she genuinely didn't understand the impact that life had had on me so far.

The nights before I was due to see her, I would begin to feel sick with worry. My parents told me it would be fine once I got there and that I should give it a try, but I was just so full of fear that I wanted to stay where I was, where I knew I was definitely safe.

Of course, there had been times when I had fun with my mother, when everything went alright and we enjoyed our time together. But these times were often overshadowed by my anxieties, and in between them were days when I found it just too hard to rebuild a relationship with my mum.

Most evenings I would struggle to sleep and go back downstairs for comfort. I remember telling my dad that I couldn't go to sleep in case James came for me. I didn't trust that she wouldn't go back to him, that she wasn't always with him, that he had some kind of hold over her. I was paranoid about it. At night, I'd lay in my bed and listen to the cars outside, listen to see if any pulled up outside our house, if there were any people around. I'd think about him and what he was doing, where he might be, whether he might be nearby, waiting for me. In a real child-like way, I'd think about the fact that he might be dead now, that something might have happened to him, but if he is, would he come and haunt me? What if I would never truly escape?

My stomach would churn and I'd start to feel sick, unsettled, uncomfortable. I'd start to become over-observant, hyper-alert, looking around my bedroom for anyone or anything out of the ordinary. Cupboards became hiding places, the cars rushing past outside became threats, and the darkness became an opportunity for anyone to jump out at me.

Every night when I went to bed, I would tell my dad, "Check on me every five minutes."

This hyper-alertness and sense of paranoia didn't let up, no matter how many times my dad tried to talk me out of it or how many times he checked on me during the night, and I was feeling sick almost permanently. Everything was a potential source of danger to my mind and I was constantly complaining that I felt unwell. We didn't know what was wrong, so Beth took me along to the doctors' surgery to get it sorted. I sat quietly while Beth explained my symptoms and behaviours, and the doctor asked me some questions. Eventually he came to his conclusion:

"It's anxiety. She'll grow out of it."

We left that day knowing what was wrong, but not what it meant to me or what treatment I should go for. And we definitely weren't offered any. All we had was the hope that he was right and that I would grow out of it eventually, if I was given enough time to process and deal with what had happened to me.

I was completely dismissed as an anxious child with no treatment for the nausea and difficult thought processes that I was experiencing. So even though I had the diagnosis, the symptoms remained, and every night brought with it the same as the one before.

My social worker came to visit our house a couple of times. He was there to make sure I was fitting in well, to see how I was coping. He would ask questions about my life here with my Dad and he would sometimes give me some simple exercises to complete, taking note of the answers I gave. He would also analyse my stories and poems, things that I had written, and ask me to talk him through some of the storylines I'd composed.

In one of these stories, there was a young girl with two houses. One was nice and one was not. In one house, the girl received food and warmth; in the other, she received none of that. I guess I was exploring things in these stories that I wasn't able to put into words otherwise.

After seeing me a few times, the social worker was asked to put together a Section Seven Report by the court, which would explore what he'd observed during the home visits, outline how I was feeling about the whole thing, and his recommendations on how to progress with my contact with my mother.

In his report, he detailed how my anxieties were very real and needed to be addressed. He also said that he wasn't entirely sure that my relationship with my mother would ever work, and that my constant fear of danger surrounding her was making it difficult to rehabilitate the relationship.

Though I hadn't read his report at the time, I know now the social worker was completely right. He knew his stuff. I was growing more and more anxious around the idea of my mother, and I was never sure if I wanted to see her. I know I made it difficult for her to build a relationship with me because of my reluctance: the short answers, timid nature and often being unsure of what involvement I really wanted with her, and after a while she gave up. She stopped calling when she said she would and didn't come to pick me up anymore. Letters stopped – I guess there was no point if I didn't reply. But I felt angry with her for lack of trying. I was scared and unsure but I still wanted her to love me. I still wanted her to try to be the mother she never had been, to prove it to me. But as time passed, we both just gave up.

I wonder, sometimes, what she must have been feeling at this point. She was incredibly young and had another child. She probably thought I was better off this way, living with my father and stepmother in Kent where I got everything I wanted. Maybe I understand it now more than I had when I was a child, but I still feel angry about it. I still feel like she never tried hard enough. I still feel like she never wanted me enough. If you love somebody you try to keep them safe, right? You certainly don't let them in harm's way.

As we drifted apart, I was scared that my relationship with my grandfather would also fall through, but thankfully it didn't. He would send me cards and I went to see him a few times, even though I no longer had a relationship with my mother. Beth would take me to visit him; she would always tell me how important she thought it was that I maintained a relationship with him because of how close we had been. I had no problem with that at all - I was always welcome in his house.

It smelt like whiskey, and whenever I smell that now, I am reminded of him like he was never gone.

FOUR

As I grew older, my symptoms fell to the side the same way my relationship with my mother did. When I was out of contact with her, I lived as care-free as everyone else seemed to be for nearly ten whole years, throughout primary and secondary school.

My dad married Beth when I was seven and I was asked to be one of her bridesmaids, wearing a burgundy dress and shoes with a little heel. I felt like good being involved in something so important. I gate-crashed their first dance: a good representation of how I had entered Beth's life a couple of years earlier. They were fun to live with: we played games, listened to music, and had dinner with Beth's - my - family each week. I had a huge Wendy house in the garden, but I didn't go in it a lot because I was scared there would be spiders inside.

In my last year of primary school, aged ten, my dad and Beth had another child.

I was beyond thrilled when they told me. I just couldn't wait to be a big sister. I knew I was going to be the best one that had ever existed. As soon as they told me, I started to plan all the things that I would do with my baby brother or sister.

We didn't know if the baby was going to be a boy or a girl, so we looked at names for both and bought neutral coloured clothing.

I remember being woken up in the night because Beth's waters had broken. My parents tried to remain as calm as possible throughout the entire thing, and they dropped me off to my Nan's around the corner, where I stayed for the rest of the night.

When I woke in the morning, it was the middle of the school holidays so I didn't have to go in. I remember eating my breakfast, unable to keep still because I was so excited about when the baby was going to come. I stared at the telephone, just waiting for it to ring so I could pick it up and find out everything about what had happened.

Eventually, after what seemed like a lifetime, my dad called to tell us that the baby was born and that it was a girl, but that there had been some complications and Beth had needed an emergency caesarean.

I wanted to see her immediately so we went that afternoon. And there she was, a tiny human lying in a hospital cot. She was wearing a beige coloured baby grow that was a little too big for her and a teeny tiny hat. I watched her sleep, her tiny hands grabbing in the air. She looked so tiny, like I could hold her in my hand, and I knew that I had been like that one day. It was so odd to look at her and think that she had been inside Beth all along.

We took her home after a while and I helped to look after her as much as I could. I fed her bottles, held her a lot, and read books to her to help her sleep. I wanted to take care of her the best I could, the way I hadn't been.

Primary school soon came to an end and I entered secondary school. I quickly made new friends and enjoyed the typical teenage things as much as I could. I found interests in English and Drama.

Unfortunately, I lost touch with my best friend from primary school. There wasn't a clear reason why; we just drifted apart. But I had made lots of other friends, including Jennie, who is now one of my best friends - a person I can turn to whenever I need advice or a chat. We met in Drama class at school and right before our GCSE performance, she broke her leg on a skiing trip in France. She phoned me straight away post-operation and told me all about it – it was enough to put me off skiing. When she came back to school she needed a wheelchair and, for obvious reasons, couldn't take part in the show. I wheeled her around school for about two months, until she was able to use crutches. We got the privilege of using the lifts at school.

Jennie and I grew very close over the years. We'd go to each other's houses, pop into town after school, give each other advice on all the important things, like how to reply to a text from a boy without seeming too needy and uncool. I even told Jennie about my childhood, and though she sympathised with me, she never judged me, saw me differently, or thought I was odd for having a Mother that seemingly wanted nothing to do with me. We always stood up for each other at school and made sure that we were both alright. We'd straighten and curl each other's hair; Jennie can always do my hair better than I can. She was always the honest friend. She will tell me if an outfit doesn't work, or if I should probably avoid this haircut in future.

I learned how to enjoy being young and carefree; I laughed with friends about boys and photos in textbooks. I was symptom-free throughout all of secondary school and it feels like, then, I was a good version of myself. I don't know why I felt so good at school in comparison to the person I'd later become and the things I would experience, I guess it took some time for my mind to catch up.

I was confident and feisty, sociable and chatty, and at sixteen I met my boyfriend, Charlie. He was friends with people I'd been friends with at school so I knew of him, but our paths had never crossed. I'd had a close friend a few years prior, and she'd been really good friends with him. She'd often be at my house after school, talking to him on my laptop, but I had no clue who he was or any conversation with him. A couple of years later I saw him in a fast-food restaurant in the town. I was at the front of the queue waiting for my food, leaning on the counter, and as I turned my head towards the door, I saw him. He was wearing his rugby kit after the morning's match and was there with some of the boys getting something to eat. Caked in mud, he stood in the centre of the group drinking from a water bottle. Brown, wet dirt sat caught in the hairs on his legs.

I left with my food and didn't think about our brief encounter for the rest of the day and, by the time I got home, I'd forgotten about it completely. Just as I was getting ready for bed, I received a message from Charlie on social media asking if it was me he'd seen today because he thought it looked like me but wasn't sure – I think he knew, really - and that I looked nice.

We continued to speak for a few weeks and at first, I was sure that it was just on a friendship basis. I was happy with the way life was going with my friends and school life, approaching exams, and wasn't really interested being in any kind of relationship, but he was persistent. Messages turned into phone calls and we'd speak every evening, usually for an hour or more, going to bed much later than we should have been and being tired for school the next day.

On the day we met properly it was PE day, which meant I had bags full of sportwear and, of course, my makeup bag for top-ups. I remember getting changed after that PE lesson and a friend who knew him well telling me "you're going to love him." It seemed everyone around me knew him but me – I wondered why our paths hadn't really crossed until now. Was it inevitable? We'd both been born in London and moved to Kent a few years apart, and part of me wonders if we were just always supposed to meet.

My friend wasn't wrong. He was the annoying type in the sense that he could get away with murder. He was annoying and took the piss out of me all the time – still does – but I forgive him in the same way I did back then. He was the epitome of a 'Cheeky Charlie' and I really liked that about him.

I was on the phone to that same friend whilst I waited for Charlie to arrive on his school bus. "Tell me everything," she'd say and "is he there yet?" After a few minutes I told her I must be off because – shit – that's his bus. I was confident then and not particularly phased by meeting a boy, but equally, I had no idea of the importance of that day.

We got together quickly and learned about each other as we went along, and silly things like foods we eat and don't eat became bigger things like how he can't bear the sound of a ticking clock, or how he can't sleep with the duvet cover around the wrong way because the buttons have to be at the bottom. Or how I didn't have a relationship with my mum.

We spoke at every opportunity and saw each other whenever we could, our parents as taxis. We would meet most days after school, and we always went to the very same bench on the river. Every time, that was our bench. He'd make up stupid songs about the things or people nearby, and I'd laugh. We spent Summers together and his friends became my friends. He lived in a beautiful village that facilitated long walks and hiding from the world under trees whilst we listened to music and spoke about all sorts of rubbish. We'd go out in a group and sit under shelters or trees, drinking beers, taking photos, singing. We didn't think about whether our relationship was serious or not or whether we'd be together in a month or a year, we just did it. We just carried on, with no idea that the years would soon pass.

Just three months into our relationship I had my end-of-school prom. I had my hair done especially for the evening and a dress I adored. Light pink, strapless, straight down. I bought shoes to match. I even fake tanned – something I never risk doing now because I can't bear the patches. I always kind of feel like I'd rather be pale than patchy. We met Jennie there and sat down to eat, the table behind us clearly full of underage drinkers and noisy party-goers causing a fuss. We didn't drink alcohol, we just ate and talked, took photos, and Jennie got to know Charlie.

He is funny, witty. He could always make me laugh and we have fun together. He is always polite, gentlemanly; the first to ask me if I'd like a cup of tea or if he can get me anything. He has been protective form the start, but even more so now we're older. He has strong morals and sticks by them very firmly. He is stubborn, tenacious, passionate, kind.

The first time he met my parents, he came home with me on the bus after school and I felt a bit nervous – my Dad is very protective, but I kind of get it. My dad was wandering around in a towel fresh out of the bath, his (always tanned) top half on show, Beth telling him to put some bloody clothes on. My little sister was five now and played with Charlie a lot; he became part of the family.

I told Charlie about my Mother and my childhood pretty early on into our time together. I have a tendency to be blasé about my circumstances as I describe them, but at the time I'd lived a good life without my Mother in it. It's just something that happened. He knew early on that I lived with my Dad and my Stepmother and the reasons for it. He knew what had happened to me but without any details; I hadn't told him about my slaughtered fish, threats of drowning or living in panic for a proportion of my childhood.

FIVE

As I settled into my new life, I still had a foot in my old one. Primarily through my grandfather, who still sent me cards and letters. I liked it. He would talk about his life, and I would write back to him, telling him all that had happened to me too. But slowly, over the years, the letters came less and less, until they stopped altogether. I later learned that he had become unwell and was unable to do things like he could before. But, because I was out of contact with my mother, I wasn't aware that he had dementia, that he was losing himself. But I never felt like he gave up on me, not when we had been so close and I had all the memories of the bond we had shared when I'd needed it most. And I understood that perhaps it was hard for him to keep contact with me when his own daughter had stopped. I often wonder if I could have tried harder with him at this time, maybe I should have tried to contact him more often, whether I had anything to do with my mum or not.

A lot of my life had moved on without her. I'd spent time focusing on my own 'stuff', on getting through school with some decent grades and to be honest, I don't remember thinking about it that often.

One afternoon during Year 10, aged about fourteen, I was in the canteen with two of my friends when I heard a ringing from my bag. I knew that nobody would ever phone me during school hours unless it was important, so I looked and saw that it was my aunt, my mum's sister. As far as I knew she didn't have a relationship with my mother either and when I moved away, I eventually lost contact with her just like I had with everyone else. We messaged each other every now and again but we hadn't spoken properly for a number of years, so it was quite the surprise to see her name on my phone.

She asked me if I was alright, and I said I was and waited for her to tell me what was up. She asked me why she didn't see me at my grandfather's funeral - she thought I would have definitely been there.

I didn't know how to answer. I felt frozen to the spot, unable to move. I felt grief rise inside me, anger, shock. I could feel my legs start to jellify as I asked her if I had heard her correctly. This can't be right. I know things are weird but surely Mum would've told me something like this? I hadn't spoken to her for about ten years but I *knew* she at least had my nan's address. I still hadn't said anything for about thirty seconds, my Aunt asking if I was OK. I started to cry, still speechless, my eyes spilling grief, anger, shock and mascara onto my school jumper.

It felt like the entire world had just stopped. I knew that it had been a while since I had last seen him, but this was the last thing I had thought had happened to him. It felt as though the last remnants of my childhood had been ripped away from me.

I couldn't find anything to say; my day had been so *normal*. The past few months had been so normal – I'd been laughing only a few seconds earlier, drinking a hot chocolate from the machine. Trying to think of the last time I saw him, I wondered what the last thing I ever said to him was, but I really don't know. I don't know if he remembered the last time he saw me either. I don't know if he remembered me at all.

I hated my mother for this. She knew how close I had been to my grandad and all I could think was is this why I lost contact with him? Because he was *dead*? Either that or he was just too ill. Whatever the reason, she had no right to rob me of going to his funeral.

Beth had always told me that no matter what happened with my mother, we would always go to my grandfather's funeral when that day came. The two of us would be civil and not let the past get in the way of me saying goodbye to someone who had been so good to me when I was a child; someone I really loved.

And yet now he was just another person who I didn't get to have closure with.

SIX

After that phone call in the canteen, I was consumed with grief. It would come at the times when I least expected it, like when I was sitting on the bus with my friends, or when I was sitting at home watching something. I would suddenly become aware that my grandfather was dead, and I would just feel hollow.

I'd experienced these feelings – this unexpected, urgent reminder that somebody is absent – for the majority of my life. I'd learned that a small part of me would always feel lonely without my Mother, no matter who I had around me, and I'd lived in the notion that no matter what great things may happen in my life, my Mother would never be there. But that was different, I grieved for what could be, not what had been. To grieve for somebody who is alive, a relationship, is a bizarre process because there is no certainty. I always felt like it was complex: she was gone, but she might come back. We might never see each other again, or we might have a relationship one day. There was a chance that, as I got older, I'd forgive her, and the waves of grief I'd experienced would become too powerful to ignore and I'd reach out for her. When it came to my Grandad, I knew I'd never have that option. It was certain.

But it wasn't just grief I was feeling. I was also so angry; angrier than I had ever been in my entire life. I felt like my mother had been vindictive in not telling me, that she had done it on purpose to hurt me. Or maybe she had simply forgotten to tell me. Either way, I needed to know.

So after about ten years of having nothing to do with my mum, I reached out to her brother who I was able to find online. In the world of social media it was easy to find him, and I knew what I wanted to say, but I kept away for a few days. I thought about what I was going to do, what this might mean for my existing relationships. I came to the conclusion that I desperately needed answers. So I sent him a message, explaining that I needed to contact my mother. I didn't explain why, and he didn't ask. He gave me her number, and so I sent her a text, too nervous to call her and actually speak on the phone.

I didn't tell anyone what I was about to do because I knew no one would truly understand and they would try to talk me out of it.

I sat completely still as I waited for a response. Seconds felt like an eternity as I stared at my phone. I knew that there was a chance that she wasn't going to reply, and I accepted the possibility that she might not want anything to do with me.

But it turned out I didn't have to wait long at all, and she replied within minutes and said that she would love to meet up with me.

I didn't know how to feel. Part of me was terrified at the prospect of seeing her again after such a long time. I had grown up without her. I knew that the conversation we were going to have wasn't going to be easy, but I knew that it was necessary. If I didn't speak to her about my grandfather, show her how angry I was at being left out of something so important, I would only continue to wonder. I knew it would drive me crazy. But there was also a part of me that was almost excited about seeing her. About wanting to see her after all this time had passed, to show her the person I had become.

Going against the wishes of everyone who loved me, I met up with her in the local park to demand explanations. Charlie came with me so that I felt supported, as I knew that every single person in my family would become frustrated with me. He walked with me to the park and went off to the gym whilst I met my mum. When I saw her, the first thing I thought was how little she had changed since I had last seen her. The second thing I thought was this was the woman who had robbed me of the opportunity to say goodbye to my grandfather.

I raised my voice at her, asking her why she had made that choice, why she had chosen to not include me in something so important. She didn't have any answers for me, couldn't say anything. She told me that she didn't know. She thought I was better off with my father, that she hadn't wanted to have any contact with me for my own safety. She cried, I didn't.

I left enraged. I left disappointed. I left having given up on the idea of my mother for a second time. I wondered how many more times this was going to happen.

She hadn't given me what I'd needed, and I wasn't surprised. She had never given me what I needed.

All I could think about as I made my way home was of other people's mothers. The friends I had, they all had such close relationships with their mothers. They told their mothers secrets and shared their fears with them, went shopping with them, knew that their mothers were there for them no matter what happened. I didn't have that, and I never would.

I knew I needed to tell my dad what had happened and that terrified me. After all, if I had told him what I was planning to do, he might have told me that it wasn't going to work out the way I wanted it to. He would have talked me out of it, told me not to go. Now I was going to break his heart.

He was sitting in the living room on the computer when I got home. Beth was out, which made it easier - at least I only had to tell one person, not two.

I was shaking, from what I had just done and what I was about to do. I told him I had something to tell him. He looked at me oddly; we never really spoke about things. We tended to save that for our friends, not our family. He asked me what was wrong, and then I just told him.

At first, the words were stuck in my throat, unable to come out, but once I forced them to come out, they just didn't stop. Deep down, I knew that my dad wasn't going to stop loving me because of what I had done, but I knew that it was going to hurt him.

He was silent after I told him. He didn't look at me, just stared at the wall by his computer screen trying to make sense of what he was told. He asked me why, and I told him exactly why, about my grandfather, the call in the canteen, my anger and grief, my need for answers.

He didn't say anything after that. I left the room.

The following days were lonely after that conversation. I knew that my father was hurt by it and Beth was furious. He had, of course, told her what had happened in conversations that I wasn't privy to, and she had taken it as a betrayal to everything she had given me.

The house felt odd for a while after that, as though people were constantly talking about me. I felt completely isolated, like nobody understood what I had done. Like nobody wanted to understand what I had done. I think the world wanted to see it as a binary, that me and my mother were completely separate and that there was no need to go back to her, but our relationship was more complex than that.

Soon after that day, my dad asked me if he could speak to me about something. I immediately became nervous and followed him into the garden where he lit a cigarette. I could see the very serious expression on his face and tried to work out what this could be about, but I had no idea.

He kept looking at me and then away from me, as though he couldn't look me in the eyes. And then he came out with it: "We're having another baby."

My heart pounded with joy. This was absolutely not what I expected this conversation to be.

When my brother was born, I cried my eyes out. I was old enough to really appreciate it this time – when my sister was born, all I thought was how cool it was to have a sister, but now, at seventeen, I could appreciate the whole process. It was overwhelming and emotional: he was tiny, warm, and so unexpected.

He came home and Charlie came to meet him, holding his tiny squishy body in his arms. I fed him, cuddled him, played with him, just like I had my sister. I enjoyed having a baby in the house again and my siblings could always cheer me up if I needed it. Having achieved good GCSE results and finishing school on a high, I managed to get myself a job working in marketing, something creative like I had always wanted to do. I'd always written stories and could very often be found with a pencil in my hand as a child, so a creative career sounded great to me. It was hard to adjust to working full time at first, but I managed to get to grips with everything. I was content and ambitious – for a while. But eventually the symptoms I had experienced as a child reared their ugly heads once more.

SEVEN

I began to cry a lot and wanted to sleep for most of the time. I didn't have much energy and felt lethargic and grumpy. But instead of the anxious thoughts about James that I had when I was younger, my thoughts turned even darker. I began contemplating about the nature of my existence, of all our existences, of whether or not there was a purpose to anything that we did. I began to focus on all the bad things in the world that were around me, like the terrorism that was constantly taking over the news, war, disease, famine, the fact that there were hundreds of children in the world suffering in the same way that I did – and worse.

While I was at work it wasn't so bad, I guess because I had other things to distract me. The constant tasks I was given, the back and forth of the work day, they all served to pull my thoughts to the side. But when I'd come home, I would feel exhausted, and I would often cry until I went to sleep.

Charlie would try to cheer me up during these times. He tried his best to understand what I was experiencing, but neither of us could really understand it at all. Jennie would come over with snacks and watch television with me. We wouldn't say much, but it was nice to be around someone even if they didn't say a single thing. I couldn't concentrate well at all and my appetite was inconsistent and unstable – as was my sleeping pattern. I could barely sleep, spending most nights awake, staring at the ceiling, unable to stop all the invasive thoughts in my head. Being tired made it all so much worse and I felt like I couldn't cope with normal situations.

One Saturday morning during this time, I received a call from my aunt – the same woman who had told me about my grandfather's passing. Charlie had stayed over and we'd not long been up and were both getting dressed and as I saw the phone ring, I just knew something was wrong. This poor woman had become the bearer of bad news.

"I didn't know if you'd want to know, but I thought you had a right to. Your mum had a stroke. Yesterday. She collapsed in the shopping centre."

She was 37 at the time, my mum, and I hadn't seen her since that time in the park – a few years ago now. I didn't know what state she was in or how unwell she was, only that she'd had a stroke.

I knew I had two options. I could either leave it and hope that she was alright, or I could go and see her. I didn't want to, not after what had happened last time, but I kept thinking about my grandfather, about how I hadn't been able to have closure with him, not being able to say goodbye, and I knew that I would regret this if I didn't go.

I told my family this time and they agreed that it was the best thing to do.

So I asked Charlie if he would take me. We both got into his car and sat quietly for most of the thirty minute journey. Isn't it strange that, for all that time, my Mum had lived only thirty minutes away – forty at a push – and yet I never saw her?

On the way there I phoned the hospital and asked them what ward she was in. As we pulled up to the hospital Charlie told me that he wouldn't come in with me, to give me and my mother some time, but that he'd wait outside and I could come and get him at any point if I wanted to. My stomach felt odd, twisted, as if I'd eaten something bad.

I made my way to the ward slowly, wondering if this was the right choice with every footstep. My mother's bed was the first in the ward, and I saw her immediately as I stepped in.

She didn't say anything, and neither did I. She looked at me as if I was someone she saw every day, until I sat down and she started to cry. She took my hand and cried on it. We didn't say much to each other on that day, we just sat. It wasn't awkward, just quiet. I had nothing I wanted to say and I guess she didn't either.

I knew in my heart that there was never going to be a real relationship between us, and I knew in my head that there was no space for her in the life I had created for myself.

I sat until I became too uncomfortable and left to find Charlie.

There were no permanent effects from my mother's stroke. They called it 'bad luck'.

I left to find Charlie and he drove me home.

EIGHT

It began to feel as though there was someone else in my head, controlling every facet of my emotion. This person, whoever they were, decided when I felt sad, which seemed to be all the time, and when I would feel happy, which wasn't very often. They told me all the reasons why I should be sad, reminding me, constantly, of all the reasons I was worth nothing, why no one cared about me, how little I mattered in the face of the world.

I'd been crying most mornings and evenings, especially on weekends. Lying in bed, I would turn my back to Charlie so that he wouldn't see me, but he usually worked it out. "Are you upset?" he'd ask, and I'd shake my head, saying no but meaning yes, whilst water splattered from my face onto the bedsheets. Most of the time I wouldn't talk, turn around or look at Charlie, but he was patient. I was becoming a child again in those moments. On most occasions I didn't know why I was crying and trying to explain that to another person isn't easy. He'd say, "there must be something? What is it?" and all I could respond with was that I didn't know.

I used to get frustrated with myself for crying over everything and it made me angry. I felt embarrassed about crying at work and feeling like I couldn't complete tasks sufficiently. I can remember thinking that I needed to just sort my shit out, for goodness' sake. A lot of the time there was no reason at all apart from the fact I just needed to cry, so I did. I didn't really feel anything apart from sadness or frustration; if it wasn't one of those then I probably didn't feel it, apart from on the odd occasion, usually with Charlie. It was like a part of my brain was going numb.

I was aware that something wasn't right within me but I didn't know what. I didn't want to be like this, but didn't know how to not be like it.

As well as the dark thoughts that I'd started to experience – about having a complete lack of purpose, or the fact that I thought the world was actually a horrible, horrible place, I also became unbearably anxious about almost everything – especially my relationship.

I would lie awake at night, engulfed in thoughts about Charlie deciding that he didn't love me anymore, and what I would do if something happened to him. I would consider many scenarios in great depth, whilst he lay next to me completely oblivious (or asleep) and throughout the course of the night I've examined scenarios in which he's decided that he doesn't want me anymore, left me, left the country and been involved in various freak accidents. I became convinced that something would go wrong somewhere: he'd either leave me or die. It absolutely consumed me, and I remember watching him and considering the possibility that it could be the last time I ever saw him. I would watch his chest for breath and consider over and over whether there will come a point at which I've just put him through too much. And that will be it.

But most days I ask him if he still loves me and the answer is always the same: yes.

NINE

I felt like this for a few months, letting it all snowball over me, until I finally realised that this wasn't going to get fixed on its own. There was something wrong and I needed help. So I made an appointment with the doctor.

As soon as he asked how I was my eyes started to fill up again almost instantly and before I knew it I was revealing everything.

It's not easy to verbalise such intense emotions, but I think my body language and behaviour did it for me anyway. My body was able to get across how I was feeling far better than my words could, shaking and struggling through lack of food, water and sleep, in a similar way to how I imagine it did when I was a child. My eyes were pouring salty droplets onto my un-made-up face and I could taste the salt as they trickled into my mouth, just like they had been for the last six weeks. I can remember looking at the floor for the majority of the conversation and thinking about what an ugly crier I am but the fact that I couldn't give a toss. The patterns on the carpet made my eyes go funny.

My body shook uncontrollably as if fevered, and I felt like a child post-tantrum: when their eyes are simply exhausted, puffy and red, and their breathing takes a bit of time to fall back into rhythm.

The Doctor told me that he thought I was suffering from depression. He gave me the phone number for a local therapy service with the NHS, but it was a self-referral system: I had to phone them myself. As soon as I left the room I decided that I was pretty sure I wasn't going to do that.

I was terrified of the label: within minutes of speaking to a Doctor about my symptoms, I was suddenly a depressed person. I was mentally ill.

I naively thought that it would go away if I ignored it and left it for a while, even though I had tried that for a few months. I convinced myself it was a phase, that I didn't need any help, that therapy was out of the question.

Two more months passed with no improvement and it became apparent that this wasn't what it was like to lead a life. I knew that it wasn't normal to feel this way all the time. But was this what it was going to be like for me for the rest of my life? That I would cry every day until I was old and that was just the way life was going to be now.

These thoughts would often cause me to panic and, eventually, resulted in me scrambling through my purse for the telephone number the doctor had provided me. I phoned them twice and hung up twice. I couldn't go through with it. Did I really need *therapy*? I didn't want to need therapy, it felt so stereotypical of my circumstances, but it was the only hope I had. So I went out into the garden and waited a few minutes before phoning for a third time and this time, I waited for a response. I lit a cigarette as a lady answered the phone and asked how she could help me. Shivering in the cool air, I told her that my doctor had given me this number. I didn't know what else to say. She told me that was fine and said that we would arrange a telephone questionnaire, where I would be asked some questions which would determine whether I *qualified* for therapy sessions.

We arranged to have another call for the following week, on which I would have a telephone interview. Thankfully, everybody was out of the house at the time of the call and I sat on the sofa, anxiously counting down how long I had, minute by minute, until this person would call me and ask me hundreds of questions about why I found living so difficult. I didn't know if I was going to be able to answer them, and I didn't even know if I was to meet the criteria for therapy. What if they told me that I wasn't that bad? That I could live with it? What if they said that they understood but there were other people who were going through worse things who needed it more than I did?

In the end after all my frantic overthinking, there were actually only about six or eight questions and they weren't too intrusive.

I had to answer most of them on a numerical scale – on a scale of one to ten, how well did I sleep, how anxious did I feel? How often? Did I have an appetite? Did it make me not want to leave the house? Did it interfere with my day-to-day life? What was the cause?

On a scale of one to ten, how much did I feel like hurting myself?

TEN

I was offered six therapy sessions after the call. Six sessions on a Tuesday morning, before work, which would help me to understand and manage my depression.

I just had to hope that it would work.

I had kept everything in for such a long time, and if I was honest, it was because nothing had bothered me for so long. Yes, there had been the grief about my grandfather's death and the anger for my mother, but otherwise, I had lived a fine life. The trauma had been blocked out, and now it was all coming back.

So I tried my best to talk about everything. My therapist listened intently while I explained what I'd experienced as a child, the symptoms I was experiencing now, the hole that was emerging where my mother should be. She was calm, gentle, empathetic.

At first, I didn't say much. There were just some

things that I physically couldn't say. I included all the things I could remember – which actually wasn't much. I began to find it frustrating that my brain had blocked out a large proportion of my memories. I didn't understand how I could be so affected by things I couldn't even remember properly.

My therapist told me that she thought it was clear that I was experiencing anger about what had happened to me and that I felt a sense of injustice. Here was this man that had had such a negative impact on my life and had gotten off with so little punishment. I was unable to go on with my life the way he had.

After each session, I would complete the same questionnaire that I'd answered on the telephone, my progress monitored each week to see if I was improving. Every week, she would ask me if I felt like hurting myself and I would always tell her that I just didn't care anymore. Not that I wanted to hurt myself, but I didn't care if I did. I recalled driving home one day on the previous week and thinking that I couldn't care less whether I crashed my car into a tree or made it home. I didn't even care enough to panic anymore; I'd either make it or I wouldn't.

She told me that this was OK because I didn't feel like I deliberately wanted to take action to hurt myself, so I probably wasn't going to at the moment. I questioned whether the tree thing was normal if she's dismissed it – maybe it's something else that comes with adult life – but I knew deep down that it wasn't.

The process was tiring and I found it so draining and exhausting but I just wanted it to work, so I tried to stick with it as much as I could. I knew that if I wasn't in it, it wasn't going to work. And I thought that it was. Being able to talk about all these things, bring them to light in such a way, meant that I was finally giving voice to the things that lived inside me.

But, just as I started to feel like I was making a bit of progress, everything went downhill just before my sixth session. Just talking about what had happened to me wasn't enough. It brought everything to the surface without giving me a way to deal with it. It began to fester, play with my mind. I began to feel more unsettled, unnerved, unstable. I was discharged from therapy – my six weeks were up.

ELEVEN

I was zombie-like, staring ahead into empty space. My eyes were open, but I wasn't looking at anything. I felt numb to the world, to myself.

There was an unusual, urgent sensation making its way around my body; something that I didn't recognise – it was different to the other things I'd been experiencing recently. I'd been low, tearful, sensitive, emotional, unstable, but I hadn't really been anxious. Not properly. I could feel the adrenaline sweeping through each limb forcing my body to shudder, my heart palpitating and causing distinct pains in my chest. I could imagine my intestines knotting as my stomach fluttered, nauseous, but whilst I could physically feel the panic inside me, it was as if I wasn't present in my body. I couldn't hear anything, I couldn't do anything, I couldn't think about anything. I had tunnel vision; everything around me had drowned out as my fight or flight mechanism kicked in, pressing me to focus on the intense feeling of dread that was gradually taking over until it gained complete control and suddenly all my senses were sharpened. I was hyper-alert; I'd gone from feeling virtually nothing, to absolutely everything.

I can't remember what triggered me, or if there even was anything that triggered me. Maybe it was the therapy sessions, maybe it was my life, memories, maybe it was just me.

Unable to sleep, I'd gone downstairs for a cigarette with Charlie and thankfully, nobody else was home. I held onto the bannister when walking down, trying hard not to slip. My body felt like it didn't belong to me, like someone else was controlling it, and I was just a puppet along for the ride. With every step I took, the pressure inside my head built until I was sure I was going to explode.

By the time I got into the kitchen, I was under attack: my thoughts viciously convincing me that there was no way that I was able to live. That this wasn't the life I wanted, that this was my life, that this was the life I was always going to have. I was corrupting myself, unable to see light from dark, encouraging myself and manipulating, persuading myself that I couldn't live this life any longer.

It was like everything had been building in my silence throughout the duration of the evening and in the days leading up to it, until I eventually exploded into tiny shards on the kitchen floor.

I became desperately hysterical, terrified of myself. My internal monologue had morphed into somebody I didn't recognise. She was harsh, threatening, aggressive. I felt dangerous, like I didn't know what I'd do next. I was completely and utterly terror-stricken by myself.

I stood on one side of the central island in the kitchen, Charlie on the other. I kept moving away from him, and he kept following me, like we were playing some sick version of a children's game. My eyes leaked fury, my body shook. I was shouting and crying, chaotic, telling Charlie that I couldn't do it anymore over and over, as if he couldn't hear me. I don't know how long I went on like this for.

Charlie held me while I struggled, distraught, desperate, until eventually, I became too tired to move anymore.

My body was weak. I felt just like the younger version of me, the sad little girl who didn't know what to do but just survive.

Having lost all energy and life within me, I had no choice but to be still. I lit a cigarette, my hands shaking. Charlie clung to me, as if I'd completely shatter if he let me go. Like I'd fall to ash on the concrete. It was like he was holding my limbs together, puppet-like, limp.

I remember him holding my face and telling me forcefully that he loved me, and I could see how desperately he wanted me to know. He cradled me whilst I tried to sleep, tears falling from my swollen eyes onto his mascara covered chest. I cried until I fell asleep, whilst he lay awake just in case.

TWELVE

When I woke up the next morning, my entire body hurt. I phoned my work and told them I felt too sick to come in. It felt like I was going to break at any moment, like I might snap with any wrong move.

I knew that I needed to get to someone who could help because if anything like last night happened again, I didn't know what I might do. I didn't trust my own judgement. I phoned the surgery as soon as I could. The phone rang and I prayed that someone would pick it up, soon, quickly. The receptionist answered after what might have been four or five rings, and asked me how she could help.

I explained my situation from the night before and she gave me an appointment for thirty minutes later. I drove to the surgery myself and waited in the reception area, waiting to be called out. I kept thinking about what might happen when I got into the doctor's room and I was just terrified of being sent away. All I could think of were those asylum stereotypes I had been brought up with, the kind of visual images from films and TV shows that showed a world that terrified me.

The doctor came out into the waiting room, called my name, and I moved in his direction.

He asked me if I was alright, and I just looked at him blankly. I tried to gather my thoughts so that I could tell him what was happening in some kind of logical sense. I wanted desperately to tell him that I felt as if I'd been overtaken by something, but the thought of having to go to a hospital stopped me. It terrified me to think that I would have to spend time there, that I would have to stay there, trapped. Labelled as unstable and ill.

I was willing to try anything at this point but the thought of being on medication was still scary.

I'd heard bad things about medication – people getting addicted, symptoms worsening before improvement. I was worried that I wasn't going to be able to function without pills, that I would become dependent on them, that they would come to define my life.

But I felt that this was the only other option, that if the therapy hadn't worked and I didn't want to go into hospital, this was what I needed. So I was prescribed an SSRI (selective serotonin reuptake inhibitor) type of medication called Sertraline.

I rushed to the pharmacy with my prescription. I was past the point of caring if anybody saw me; what difference would it make to me now anyway? My sole focus was keeping myself on the tightrope and I didn't care who saw. I took the first tablet as soon as I got home and fell asleep soon after.

My parents hadn't wanted me to start taking Sertraline. They were worried about the effects it might have on me, of the addiction, the dependency, the numerous side effects. Beth told me that it was only going to work because I wasn't going to be able to feel anything at all. I don't think either one of them understood the need to go on medication, but for me, it was blindingly clear. It's hard to explain a panic attack.

I had become so uncomfortably aware of my mental illness on that night. I'd learned what it was capable of and how it could take over me, the poisonous thoughts that it would feed me. I now knew that, at any moment, I could enter a state of immediate and irrational panic.

So Sertraline it was.

I quickly discovered that my body wasn't keen on the substance I was forcing into it. My fingers tingled every second I was awake and when I wasn't, I would wake up regularly to rush to the bathroom ready to vomit. I couldn't eat, I'd fall asleep mid-sentence, disturbed again an hour later by overwhelming nausea and a complete sense of disorientation.

Each night I went to sleep in the hope that the morning would be better, an improvement on today. It usually wasn't. I still felt sick, weak and mad.

After a few days of this, I started Googling what I was experiencing - obviously. I scoured the internet, looking for anything that could help me. I fell onto forums and found people who were like me, who were experiencing the same thing I was. And all of them said to stick with it because it would get better. And perhaps that worked for them, but with every passing day, I just couldn't. I felt worse.

One of the longest times I was awake whilst on Sertraline happened when Charlie came home from work one evening. He was armed with his usual 'care package', as he called it. Chocolates, smoothies, sweets, fruit. I never ate any of it. I was grateful for all his efforts, I just couldn't eat anything. My stomach refused to keep anything down, no matter how small or sweet it was.

It meant that he'd eat dinner whilst I slept or, sometimes, just watched him. Today, whatever he was eating required a steak knife. It had become the norm for me now to have thoughts that were dark - they normally came and went quickly, passing through, but this one lingered. All I could think about was the knife: the fact that I could just stab myself if I wanted to.

Charlie was talking to me, but I wasn't listening. On the information leaflet that had accompanied the medication it stated that a common side effect was suicidal thoughts. This struck me as quite ridiculous, frankly – "here's an antidepressant! It will make you stop wanting to live."

I became consumed by this strange infatuation I had with the steak knife.

I was aware that it would take a while for me to feel the benefits of taking antidepressants, as this was something the doctor had made very clear. But there was a difference between talking about something and going through it.

I was either feeling suicidal or nothing at all. My body was weak and dirty, still tingling as the chemicals made their way through my blood. I just wanted to be myself again. The thoughts I was experiencing whilst medicated were much worse than when I wasn't, and I was so sick of feeling sick. I couldn't lead a normal life because at least one of the two daily tablets would knock me out. I couldn't bear another day of persistent nausea, of waking up at four thirty-seven every single morning.

I went back to the doctor after only a week and

told him that there was no way he would get me to take a single dose more. I was done. My parents and Charlie supported my decision to stop taking my medication. Seeing me in the state I was in can't have been easy for anyone, and I truly felt that Sertraline was making me worse. I didn't know what I was going to do next, I just knew I couldn't continue like this.

I explained the side effects that I'd been experiencing to the doctor and that I'd felt much more unstable over the last week than I ever had before. I told him that I didn't trust myself when I was taking the meds, but that really was only half of it. The unbearable side effects had gotten the better of me and I couldn't face another day of it.

He told me that he thought I'd had a bad reaction to Sertraline and asked me if I wanted to try something else.

Absolutely not.

I wanted my life back. The last week had felt like a complete blur and yet I could remember it all too well. The doctor assured me that reactions to medication weren't usually so extreme and that I just needed to find the right one for me, but I didn't want to.

I left the surgery in a hurry. I wanted to forget that any of this had happened at all. I wanted to start again and go back to normal. I wanted to be normal. I wanted to experience the joy I had felt when I'd first met Charlie and he'd charmed me with useless scientific facts that he'd learned in school that day – something about atoms. I wanted to go into work without falling apart at the first hurdle, to take part in meetings and to think creatively. I didn't want to look back on life before all this with longing, with hope; I wanted to live it.

I wanted to hug Charlie, tell him it was all over, tell him I was sorry for making him go through everything the way we had. I wanted to have a shower, wash everything away as if it would all roll off my body and fall into the plughole, just as the water would. I wanted to get in my car, drive it without my hands shaking, listen to pop songs on the way to wherever I was going.

I just wanted to get through a single day without crying. I wanted to laugh, to smile, to be sad because of something normal, to be angry, to enjoy myself. I wanted to feel these things the way I had before.

I went back to work with a cup of tea waiting for me. I cried at the sight of it and remember the frustration I had with myself because of this. Why was I crying? I didn't know. There was no answer to any of it, no answer to anything I was feeling. I just wanted to be able to shut it all out, to put a lid on it, close off the tap, make it all end. I couldn't help but think of all the time I had spent at school, of how I had been okay, of how I had been fine, and now it was all just so different.

I still cried most mornings just as I had before, but I knew I didn't want to end up completely broken in the way that I had been the previous week, when I was taking Sertraline. I had to keep myself afloat; I couldn't do it again. The routine certainly helped and I managed to keep myself going for a few months. I remembered all the things I had longed for the day I stopped my medication, and now I had them. I didn't only see my boyfriend when I woke up for five minutes, I didn't live on smoothies. I could have smoothies out of enjoyment, not because they were my only option. It's fair to say that this gratitude kept me going for a period of time, and I only cried sometimes. The capacity for different emotions living in my brain had grown substantially, and when I felt things, I felt them entirely. I'd cry when somebody was nice to me, when I felt grateful or when I felt happy. But it also meant that when I felt low, I felt really low. The only way I could get around this was taking every day as it came, in whatever form it came. Some days would be just as bad as before, and some would be OK.

THIRTEEN

Winter came and the days grew dark, cold, more difficult. I felt like the past year had been particularly unforgiving, but I had no sense of hope for the future. I felt like another mental downturn was waiting for me at some point. To distract myself, I decided that having a hobby or something to focus on would benefit me. I could focus on that instead of waiting for the cracks to show again, for me to fall into them.

I'm not really sporty or academic or musical - I needed something that would allow me to be creative but not pressured, something that I could do when I felt lethargic, something that would keep my brain busy without being overwhelmed.

I didn't know what I was looking for until Jennie asked me about blogging. She read them and watched people vlog on YouTube. She enjoyed her time with them, said that it made her feel as though they were friends. I watched a few myself too, and liked seeing people talk to me like they knew me, and the intimacy of it. But I couldn't do it myself. There was no way I was going to film myself and put it on the internet for everyone to see.

But the thought stayed in my head, of blogging. It was after Jennie had given me a book to read, one by Zoella, a YouTuber who had turned to writing fiction, that I made the decision to start a blog. Maybe writing would help my anxiety too.

Two days before Christmas, I decided that it would be worth a try, to start a blog, and that maybe I had more to say than I thought. I've always written ever since I was small – ever since I moved in with my dad. I decided that it didn't really matter if nobody else read it, I just wanted to write. So I thought of a name for my blog – Little Thoughts – and that's what it would be. Random, small posts covering whatever I fancied, whenever I fancied. No pressure from anyone, not even myself.

I wrote my first post on the same evening, introducing myself as the anxiety-ridden person that I was. I didn't try to exaggerate the things that I went through, and neither did I try to make them appear to be smaller than they were. I was honest, more than I've been before, and I sent it out there into the internet.

I remember feeling nervous about it at first. I didn't know what to expect, and the thought of putting myself out there with such honesty, such openness, was terrifying. I had only told Charlie and Jennie about the blog, not wanting to tell anyone else, not wanting to see what they had to say about me.

But I'd given myself an outlet, something that I could do, something that could distract me.

Christmas soon passed and I was pleased to see the back of it. I felt like I had to perform when it came to Christmas. You have to go to parties with family and friends, embrace the 'Christmas spirit', drink alcohol and smile and be happy. I just found it exhausting – and fake.

I wrote another post on mental health, urging people to allow themselves to feel whatever they needed to over the Christmas period, to remove the pressure, cut themselves some slack, know that they're not the only one. Once I made this blog post, I created social media profiles to promote my blog posts but remained anonymous. I wanted to be able to write whatever I wanted without anyone finding out it was me. The distance allowed me to write without any kind of reservations. I could just write.

As time went on, I wrote more posts. It felt good to get myself out there in this way, and it felt even better to know that I was helping other people. I wrote most days and had posts scheduled for weeks in advance, my head full of ideas and my fingers desperate to type them. The more I posted, the more people began to follow me online. People started commenting on my posts, letting me know that they felt the same, that they could relate in some way, and thanking me for writing it. I was building relationships with people who understood what I was experiencing and also wrote blog posts about their mental health experiences.

I realised how important this was, to reach out to people, make them feel like they're not alone, so I made the decision to reveal myself. I put my name to the blog, put a photo to the profiles, and people supported my decision to do so. I felt like I had taken an important step forward.

FOURTEEN

Feeling a bit more settled and having gained some purpose back from blogging, I booked a long weekend away in Barcelona as a surprise trip for Charlie's birthday. I was excited and looking forward to it – I just couldn't wait to see his face when I told him. I'd booked it about five months in advance and not telling him about the trip was so difficult – I shared everything with him and keeping this secret had been almost impossible.

At the time of booking the trip, all I could feel was excitement. I wasn't worried about going away and I'm guilty of making decisions for the future without thinking about what I might be feeling like then. I knew I was still experiencing high levels of anxiety but I was somehow convinced that this would be fixed in time: yes, I'll be able to attend your party in three months' time, I'll be right as rain and anxiety-free by then, I'm sure.

And for a while I was. A week before the trip, Jennie came over to my house – as she usually did on a Wednesday evening – and I was sharing my excitement with her, packing for the trip. We were choosing day outfits and evening outfits and beach outfits, deciding whether I'd need a hairdryer, making sure I had my passport in a safe place.

I hadn't been on a plane for a few years, but Charlie and I had been away together many times before and had some happy holidays. We drove to the South of France and didn't have a single wobble on the ten-hour journey – not even with the disgusting sandwiches we'd bought, getting lost or the broken satnav. We took everything as it came and I wasn't anxious for any of it. We'd even been pulled over by French police on the way and we got lost, and there were no anxieties even then, and that trip had only been a year or so before this one. But I was a good version of myself then. So I didn't even think about any potential anxiety on the week leading up to our flight to Barcelona - not until the night before.

I was at Charlie's house having dinner with him and his mum, who was going to drive us to the airport in the morning. We'd been talking about where we'd like to go when we got there and practicing mispronounced Spanish. I was thinking about the makeup I was going to buy when I got to Sephora, dragging Charlie around with me with the promise that we could go to the beach afterwards. All I felt was excitement about all the things that we were going to do. I didn't even think, for a second, that something might happen to make that change.

We sat down to eat, and that was when it happened. I always know it's coming because of the nausea. I made it through dinner but I didn't eat much at all. I could feel myself starting to sweat, so I took myself upstairs to have a sit down and get myself back on track. I started to shake and couldn't see properly – this always happens when I'm sick with worry. I went into the bathroom and threw up twice. My body was shaking but sweaty, clammy. I was full of fear – the kind of fear that was urgent and unforgiving. It was the kind of fear in which every part of my body was refusing to make another move. I felt frozen, like I was standing in front of my biggest fear.

Whenever I get like this, every part of my body is telling me that I should get out as soon as possible. It can feel like I'm punishing myself for not doing what my mind and body wants. If I continue to do something that my brain doesn't want me to do, it will reject food. It will reject sleep. It will affect my breathing. I'll become dizzy, I'll cry.

I made Charlie drive me home. I wasn't even embarrassed about it anymore; I just had to get out of the house. There was absolutely no way that I was flying to Barcelona in the morning, not a single chance. Beth tried to calm me down when we got in the house while Charlie stood, helpless.

Of course he really wanted to go, and I felt so bad about it. I told him to go without me, that he had to go. I didn't want him to miss out on something just because of this thing that I had. I felt like he had already missed out on so much. A normal relationship, a normal girlfriend. I wanted him to go.

I was crying hysterically, unable to catch a breath or understand what anyone was saying. Everything just felt like it was underwater. I didn't care about the money I'd spent on the trip or the fact that I had actually always wanted to visit Barcelona, like Beth kept telling me. I just wanted to stop feeling this way. I just wanted everything to stop.

This panic attack lasted for hours until I eventually exhausted myself into being unable to do anything except lay quietly.

I still get upset about that night. I feel guilty and embarrassed and upset at the way I behaved. I feel bad about how I told Charlie to just go without me.

When the morning came, I was able to think more clearly but it's safe to say I was still exhausted. Knowing that I'd regret not going on this trip if I gave up on it, and that I needed to do this for Charlie, I got dressed, shaky, picked up my handbag, and got in the car. I didn't say anything for the entire journey – I don't think anyone did.

When we arrived at the airport, Charlie took our bags out of the boot and we waved Beth goodbye, who had driven us. We stepped onto the escalator to go up into the airport from the drop-off area and I was focused only on getting to the top.

I had decided the best way to do this was to break every single section of this trip down into tiny steps, which is something that Charlie always suggests to me when I'm faced with a situation that I may find difficult. When I couldn't face the day, he'd tell me to just focus on getting out of bed first. Then I can eat breakfast, then I can get dressed. I focus on one thing at a time and not what will come next. So I focused on getting to the top of the escalator, walking into departures, then I would check in, then I would go through security, then I would eat something.

Preparing to go through security, we picked up clear plastic bags for our travel-size toiletries, but I could feel that my stomach was still unsettled so I was stashing the bags into my handbag in case I needed them later. Waiting in the security line, holding onto my mini shampoos, I was vomiting into the little clear bags and stuffing them into the bin nearby, trying to be as discreet as possible for the poor holidaymakers next to us who were definitely getting more than they had bargained for. My next focus was getting through the security machine, which, of course, beeped because I hadn't taken my earrings out.

I don't remember the wait to get onto the plane. I don't even remember getting onto the plane. I just remember dazing in and out of sleep while we both listened to our music, holding hands the whole journey. I was woken by the sound of the pilot telling us that we'd soon be landing in sunny Barcelona, as well as the local time and weather. We had done it. I'd gone from absolute refusal only a matter of hours ago to landing in Barcelona. Now that it was done, I didn't feel anxious at all. As soon as I looked at Charlie's smiling, excited, forgiving face, I knew I was alright. His face is safe.

The anxiety seemed to have passed and I was ready for holiday mode, but even though it was no longer there, I still felt like it could come back at any point. It springs up without warning, so I spent a lot of the trip on high alert.

After collecting our luggage, we stepped out of the airport into the warm Spanish air and lit cigarettes before piling into a taxi to our hotel. It was a short journey and we admired the views on the way, and we were alright.

That was the best holiday I've ever had. We were happy and comfortable and together. But it was more than just enjoying myself. It was the fact that I had done it. Every bone in my body had wanted me to give up on the idea of the trip, but I did it. Charlie often says he'd like to go back and that it was one of his favourite holidays so far – it was one of mine too.

We went on holiday again that year. We were

attending a wedding in Cyprus and while I now knew that I could get on a plane because I had done it only a few months ago, I still knew that my anxiety would come back at any point with little warning. It made me feel unsure of myself, and I could never tell just how much I could trust any sense of safety. And, because it was a two-week trip, I worried that something might happen when I was there, when I was unable to be at home, with all the security that lent me.

Leading up to the Cyprus trip, I could feel myself starting to go downhill again. I kept thinking about the night before Barcelona, how my body had yet again been taken from me, ripped away from me. I wasn't in control of it, and it had made sure I had known that. I was scared of myself again. I was throwing up every day and had been for months.

We left for Cyprus early in the morning, and I managed it in the same way I had managed Barcelona. Step by step, bitesize chunks, but this time with the reminder that I'd done it only a few months ago. I can remember standing in the check-in queue and feeling fine, feeling happy, wondering what had happened to me. I wondered when the anxiety would come – it was inevitable that it would at some point. This in itself can be anxiety-inducing: anxiety formed from anxiety itself.

I slept on the flight, my hand in Charlie's, just like before. It was a lovely family trip and the wedding was beautiful, but I was aware that I wasn't myself for much of it.

FIFTEEN

Sometimes when I wear my hair curly, I think I look just like how I remember my mum. I had a passport-style photo of her in her twenties which sat in the top of a blue folder holding court-related paperwork. I sometimes looked at it, to remind myself of what she used to look like. I don't know where it is now, lost somewhere. That photo always made me think that I should know who she is, that the reason I owned this photo was because I knew this woman. But I didn't.

I didn't know what she was like, what her favourite food, colour, film, song was. I didn't know where she lived, what her house was like, what she liked to watch in the evenings. I didn't know if she had the same post-traumatic problems that I have; if her mind had struggled to process the events and people that we encountered in my early childhood. I didn't know if she liked to read and write like I do, if she was where I got my creative side from. I didn't know what I got from her, if anything.

The intensity of these wonderings fluctuated; sometimes it was merely a curiosity, sometimes an all-consuming, burning desire to know more. There was a gap in my biology that I wondered if I'd ever fill. Would I ever learn to live with it, happy in the knowledge that I am me and she is her, and that the nine months she carried me for are just a small part of a much larger picture? That the only untarnished time I had with her was the two years before she split with my father, and I don't remember those anyway. That the only true memories I have of my mother are from that rotten house with her rotten boyfriend and I knew no different, apart from some trips to the park, to my grandfather's house and some handwritten letters on coloured paper – letters that I didn't reply to.

I wanted to know what she was like as a person. I wanted to see if there would ever be a relationship between us; whether we'd ever be able to do things together as Mother and Daughter.

I had kept her phone number, from the time I had met her when I needed to ask her about my grandfather a few years earlier, so I just had to hope that it hadn't changed. I thought about sending her a message for a few days – I needed to be sure this was what I needed to do.

It was a Sunday morning when I decided to send the text, my anxious heart beating at an unhealthy rate. I asked her if she wanted to meet me for a coffee, sending the text before I could convince myself not to.

Straight away I was questioning my decision – was this the right thing to do? Was I setting myself up for a fall or would this finally provide me with what I needed? I stared at the phone, waiting for her to reply, trying not to think about the last time I had been in this situation.

She replied a few minutes later. We arranged to meet. It felt different.

I didn't know what to expect when we met up. She wore a long, light brown coat, the kind of coat I'd been wanting to buy for a while but had been worried that I might be too short for that particular style. I'm only about five foot four, whereas my mother is about five foot seven or so. Her boots matched her handbag and nail polish and she dressed the way that I wished I dressed. She dressed the way I would dress if I could get up on time in the mornings.

I wondered what passers-by thought of us together as we met. Quite often when I'm out for dinner or in coffee shops with Charlie, we look at the people around us and try and guess the relationship between them. I was certain that people would know that we were mother and daughter if they played games like that. I looked like a smaller version of her, only with a slightly bigger nose and the long, brown hair that she'd had when she was my age.

We spoke about normal things. I told her about my therapy and it turned out that she had gone through a bit of it herself, although mainly within stroke rehabilitation. We spoke about my siblings and how they were getting on with school, the fact that her other daughter, my sister, was horse-mad and rode whenever she could, and I said that I'd like to see them. I'd missed out on their lives as much as my Mum's. I didn't know them.

After we met on this occasion, we decided that we were going to meet again. My family knew about my meetings with my mother from the start this time, and they thought that I was making a mistake. My Dad told me that he would be there when it all went wrong.

I'd go to her house and have cups of tea, sometimes dinner, and she'd even cut my hair sometimes because she was a hairdresser. We laughed a lot when we were together, went shopping, bought coffees, painted our nails, ate cakes. I met my siblings and spoke to my mother about all sorts, work, friends, life, and Charlie came to visit on some occasions too. Like my dad, he was worried that I would get hurt, and I don't think he could ever forgive my mother for some things I'd been through. But he would always support me with whatever decisions I made.

I distinctly remember how protective she was of her other children, especially her daughter, and it made me think that maybe she was making up for the childhood I could have had with her. She had an opportunity to try it again. She cared about them, wanted to take care of them, made sure that their concerns and worries were heard. And it seemed like they truly loved each other. Whenever I visited her, I never sensed any kind of negativity from her to them or vice versa. It seemed like she had created something for herself that we had never had.

On one evening I was driving home and that feeling of anxious nausea – the one I know well – came over me very quickly. Thankfully I had a plastic bag. On that night, throwing up along the M25, I knew that I'd had it. Whether I wanted it or not, a relationship with my Mother would only make me ill.

It didn't feel like I imagined it would. The kind of relationship that I wanted was never going to be possible because I had missed out on too much. She tried and was a good friend to me, but I wasn't mentally capable of being mothered by her.

I just didn't know how to do it. I thought I'd be able to just jump straight in and it would all be normal because she was still my mother. I thought that by being involved in her life, and her being involved in mine, that the holes would be filled. But the problem with that was that I didn't need her to fill them in - I had to do that myself. I'd not seen her or had any contact with her for almost ten years and even as an adult it was inconsistent – on my part. I just didn't know what was best for me.

Once again, my days became consumed with leaking eyes and hiding in the office toilet.

I'd known my then-manager for a number of years, and when things got particularly tough, he told me that he'd been seeing a private therapist for a few weeks who'd helped him a lot in his personal life, and that maybe she could help me too. I was still being sick every day. I knew that I needed to do something because things were becoming very difficult again, but I needed it to work this time.

I didn't want to have to pay for it, but if that was what I needed then I knew it was a step that I was willing to take.

SIXTEEN

I stepped outside of the office and the fresh air filled my lungs. I was too nervous to call. I thought maybe she would be too busy to pick up, maybe she'd be with a client and I'd be faced with the dreaded voicemail. I hate leaving voicemails. She answered straight away.

I told her that she had been recommended by a friend, and that he thought she could help me. The words came out a lot easier than I thought they would, and before I knew it, I was telling her about all my symptoms and experiences over the past couple of years.

She told me she could fit me in that evening for a complementary session, to see if we would fit together. She emailed me her postcode and booked me in for six – unexpectedly quick, but I needed to get the ball rolling so welcomed the opportunity.

As the day went on, I grew more and more anxious

about the session. She seemed like a pleasant person, and she had been recommended to me by someone who said she was good, but I couldn't help but think about what I'd experienced before and whether this woman would be like that. I was worried that talking about everything would send me off into the downward spiral I'd experienced before, and I certainly wasn't about to pay forty pounds a week for that.

It was growing dark outside; time to go. It was late September and the air was cool. I'd looked at the journey before I'd left: it was going to take me fifty minutes to get there – all country lanes – but I remember thinking that at least it wasn't icy or foggy. I put the radio on before I set off, filling my car with voices so that I didn't have time to think about what was coming.

I arrived at the house in just under fifty minutes and parked on the driveway. It was a beautiful, homely property with warm light and two other cars on the drive and I remember thinking that she must be pretty good at what she does to be able to afford to live there. I rang the doorbell and took a step back, anxiously awaiting her response. I saw her come down the stairs in a window to the left of the door and felt my heart pick up as she came closer and closer to the door. It was as if every part of my body knew that soon, this woman would know everything about me and be able to do whatever she wanted with the information I gave her. This woman had the power – apparently – to change my life, but would she?

She greeted me at the door, asking me to come in. I followed her inside the house, unable to keep myself from looking around at the place she lived in.

She was about the same height as me with very

short curly hair, maybe in her forties or fifties. She glowed as if she'd just returned from a holiday. She led me up one flight of stairs into what must have been her working room. It had an armchair for her and a sofa for me, a fireplace and a bookshelf.

She offered me a glass of water and I sat down, holding it in my hands but not drinking it. We began to discuss why I was there: the anxiety I'd been experiencing, the crying I'd been doing, the fact that I was getting flashbacks again, all the throwing up. Once I'd explained my situation, my therapist was convinced that my diagnoses up to now had in fact been very wrong. She said that she didn't doubt that I was suffering from depression and anxiety, as previously told, but explained that they were part of something a bit bigger. She told me that it was quite clear to her that I was suffering from Complex-Post-Traumatic-Stress-Disorder and that I actually always had been.

I was completely baffled by this. PTSD was something that war heroes suffered from – people who had bravely sacrificed everything they had - not someone like me. Not someone who hasn't suffered anything comparable to what soldiers suffer. But I was wrong. She told me that anyone who has experienced trauma can suffer from PTSD, not just veterans.

My therapist explained to me that the word 'complex' highlighted the very important difference between two types of PTSD: complex PTSD occurs when a trauma goes on for a period of time, whereas PTSD generally occurs after a one-off trauma such as a car crash, an assault or an accident. She explained the symptoms to me and they seemed very familiar: episodes of losing attention or concentration and feeling somewhat removed from your body (sometimes referred to as dissociation), anxiety attacks, depression, flashbacks (physical and emotional), and physical symptoms such as dizziness, stomach pains, headaches – and of course, the vomiting.

I remember sitting while she listed the symptoms and ticking them off.

Tick, tick, tick.

SEVENTEEN

It all made sense.

Within minutes of meeting this woman, she had worked it out and knew what I was going through. She made me feel seen, justified, validated. Whilst a proper, accurate diagnosis isn't really what I grew up wanting, I knew that it was certainly going to help. It felt like now I knew what was wrong, I could properly fix it this time.

She told me that, if I wanted to, we could try a trauma therapy specific for PTSD cases called EMDR. When she explained it all to me, it sounded a bit like hypnotism and was terrifying, but I was willing to give anything a go at this point. I couldn't go on throwing up and crying every day.

EMDR stands for Eye Movement Desensitisation and Reprocessing and aims to alter the way that traumatic memories are stored within the brain. In cases of CPTSD, traumatic memories are stored in the short-term memory bank, forcing us to relive them when they're triggered. Instead of looking back on them like an image, you're back in that moment doing it all again. The therapy would attempt to move the memories into the long-term memory, reducing their impact and making them less vulnerable to triggers.

When we sleep at night and reach REM, our eyes move rapidly as our brains process the day's events. This part of the sleep cycle doesn't last long but is incredibly important, as it gives the brain a chance to file things away. EMDR therapy aims to replicate this experience. The therapist moves his or her hand in a particular way whilst you follow it with your eyes whilst conjuring up a difficult memory, emotion or experience, creating a rapid eye movement and encouraging the brain to reprocess whatever it is you're thinking of.

The problem is, to reprocess, you have to re-experience. I was warned that any physical marks or blemishes may reappear and that I would mentally be experiencing a lot of things again. She gave an example of an ex-client who was suffering from PTSD after a car accident. With EMDR therapy her mental state improved drastically but whilst going through the process, her seatbelt mark had reappeared on her chest just like it had after the accident, and this is something that I'd have to take into account if I chose to go with this type of therapy. I was aware that the brain is powerful, but I didn't realise quite how so. I'm not even going to try and say that this wasn't terrifying to me because it was, but I remember sitting on her sofa and thinking that if I did it once at the age I did it then, I could do it again now.

She also explained to me that CPTSD can usually become significantly worse when you're still in contact with the person responsible for the trauma.

It's not that I was in contact with the person who was specifically responsible for the trauma, I know nothing of James, but I guess that my mother was someone who had been involved with that. I could even argue that my mother not protecting me from trauma – and later losing any relationship we had - was traumatic in itself. It made sense: my main, most consistent difficulties had seemed to correlate with contact with her.

I knew I had an important decision to make. Would I continue to have random bouts of contact with my mother or even a more long-term relationship with her, or was I going to put my health before her in the hopes that I could heal?

I had to accept that there was always going to be a part of my brain that will perceive my mother to be a source of danger. Due to the nature of CPTSD, and trauma, it's as if part of my brain stopped developing at four years old and couldn't move on and, as a result, it's like a small part of me will always be four.

Being in contact would mean I was in contact with a permanent trigger, so I made the decision that I wouldn't have any contact with her. I just wasn't prepared to put myself in any position that could worsen my already troublesome mental state. I made my decision very quickly – probably more quickly than you'd expect – but I look back on it often. I don't regret my decision, but I think it's a shame that I had to make it in the first place. Having to accept that your biological mother is not good for you is a strange and difficult concept.

I agreed to come back and start EMDR therapy. I would assess how I was getting on week-on-week, and went back to therapy most Tuesdays for about fifteen weeks. It was winter and I cancelled some of the sessions due to fog or bad weather. Because of the drive that I needed to take to get there, I thought it wasn't a good idea to drive when I wasn't feeling too confident and the nature of EMDR meant that my eyes often struggled a bit afterwards. But I didn't find that these missed sessions stunted my progress massively and I was able to just come back the next week and pick up where we left off. I had about twelve sessions in total.

Every week, the two of us would work on a memory – the tape, the fish, behavior, abuse - and I would follow her hand with my eyes to reprocess and desensitise them, my reactions gradually improving throughout a session as we worked on the same thing, over and over. Getting someone to experience a traumatic memory once, by choice, is difficult enough, but doing the same thing over and over was incredibly difficult. There was something empowering about it though. I felt that I was becoming desensitised to some of the things that had ruled my life in such an overwhelming way, and I gradually watched the therapy whittle it away. Plus, my therapist made it very clear from the start that I would be in control of the whole process – what we did, how we did it, what I shared, what I didn't.

Those first few sessions were exhausting and my eyes struggled on the journeys home. I was concentrating as much as I could bear in each session, focusing hard on reprocessing each memory bit by bit, while facing the consequences of dredging up the trauma once again. Quite often, working on one memory would bring up another one, and it turned out that I had this entire life just sitting there, clogging up my brain like oil in a drainpipe.

As well as helping me to manage my memories and giving me the coping skills to better deal with my anxiety, EMDR therapy also changed my whole perception of the events that had led me to this point and who I was as a person. In one particular session, my whole mindset was changed just by focusing on the tiny version of me in the memory we were focusing on that session, instead of the memory itself.

Now that I had been somewhat desensitised from the memory, I was able watch it as if it was a TV show – not a TV show I'd like to watch, mind – as I followed my therapist's hands with my eyes. All sorts of things pop into your head with EMDR, as our brains tend to link one thing to another, and then to another, and then to another. This specific time, I could see myself, aged about four, looking up at me as if my child self was standing in the room in front of me. I was wearing a cute dress and had brown, bobbed hair. Big eyes. It was like the tiny me had stepped out of the memory itself and had come alive. The rest of the room was gone.

I instantly became full of kindness, compassion, protectiveness. I felt it fill my body. It was as if she'd been given a second chance – she wasn't protected back then, but now she could be. Because I could protect her. *Me*. I could protect myself.

I could feel her presence in such an overpowering way that when my therapist's hand stopped moving, I could still only focus on little me. It was hard, sitting there, to make the link between this tiny person and myself. I had to force myself to accept and understand that she wasn't there anymore, that she was gone, and had grown into me. I didn't need to feel bad for her any longer because she had turned into me, into someone with a good life, someone who was okay. She made it.

By the end of the EMDR sessions, my panic had been reduced significantly. I didn't spend every day waiting for awful things to happen, or become so exhausted from trying to control my emotions. I still had work to do though, and I had to accept that it will probably always be that way for the rest of my life. There are some things that will always be triggers for me, but now I know how to better manage my anxieties.

EIGHTEEN

I achieved and learned a lot while doing EMDR. Not only did I complete the course and reprocess some difficult memories, I managed quite a lot of other things as well. It gave me the understanding and the knowledge of my illness to enable me to work with it, to know why I was feeling anxious, and to know that it was just little Hannah inside me asking for a bit of help.

This enabled me to do things that I would have really struggled with before, like going to London, going on the tube, going away to other countries, or even just going out to eat. They were still more difficult than I felt they should be, but each time, when I could feel my anxieties coming to the surface, I would remind myself of the small part of my brain that had been stunted at four.

I felt like my quality of life had completely deteriorated when I was constantly anxious, and the number of different activities I felt I could do was gradually getting smaller and smaller. This was a really scary reality. I'd spoken to people online – thanks to my blog and social media accounts – who were so full of anxiety that they were unable to leave their houses and that terrified me. I didn't want to become that person – I didn't want it to become that bad. So I tried my best to implement all that I had learned during the therapy.

Even so, I still found some events difficult. Anything that was out of the ordinary, or that threw off my usual routine, became a source of anxiety. Rare trips to London, to a new place, staying somewhere new overnight, or even work meetings occasionally. I wasn't living in a permanently anxious state anymore, but I still didn't cope well with these types of events or occurrences and would still have to remind myself, a lot, that things are okay now.

Before the therapy, I would enable myself to cancel plans because it was much easier than having to face it. If I knew that I'd either have a panic attack or vomit, what was the point? The problem was that every time I cancelled on something and enabled my anxiety to win, to dictate my actions, I was building up an intolerance to the situations that fueled my anxiety. Every time I avoided something, I was teaching myself that there was something to be scared of; teaching myself to believe the anxious thoughts and feelings that I was experiencing. I had to remember that it was a child talking. The tiny version of me was inside overpowering my thoughts with her panic, I just had to reassure her. Teach her.

I had to learn to navigate the world with CPTSD and not let it stop me, to just let it be a part of me without dictating who I am. I had to face the things that scared me to teach myself that it was alright, that

I could get on the train, that I could be far from home, that I could be in busy venues.

One thing that helped was meditation. Lots of other lifestyle and wellbeing bloggers had spoken online about it, so I thought I'd give it a go. At first I thought it was completely ridiculous and found it difficult to focus seriously on the woman speaking to me through my headphones and focusing only on my breaths, but after a few nights of meditating before bed, I began to see its benefits.

My therapist supported it when I told her, and told me that meditation was great for anxiety as well as those who struggle to sleep, so I continued to use it. Before long, I was meditating most evenings with an app on my mobile phone and this became a bit of a safety blanket for me. I knew that it worked and would fend off the worst of my anxiety on most occasions, so whenever I was at home and started to feel myself become anxious, nauseous, shaky, I would use the app for ten minutes. Nine times out of ten it worked, so I knew I would be okay if I could do this.

I found that my tendency to expect anxiety was half the battle I was facing. Knowing that a situation is likely to cause me distress, I find that the knowledge or build-up becomes more anxiety-inducing than the situation itself. It was a constant battle, trying to fight past the pre-situation anxiety, going through the situational anxiety, learning to cope with the post-situation anxiety – the *adrenaline hangover*. It was all so exhausting.

NINETEEN

Little Thoughts continued to do well, reaching people across the globe. Some of my posts were getting more views than I had ever imagined, and the community I built around me were supportive. A beauty company decided they were going to invite me to a launch event for a new product - there was no money involved or pressure to write about anything; I just had to turn up.

This was something that I definitely would have avoided a year prior. It would have filled me with anxiety and I wouldn't have been able to do anything about it except sit at home and feel bad. But, because I was much stronger, I felt proud of myself for being invited, and excited to see some other bloggers.

The event was in London, which meant trains. I'd have to meet the other bloggers and eat lunch with them, and then I'd have to get on the train again to come home, which would take about fifty minutes.

London has always been a little scary to me, I think just because of how busy it is. If I panicked I wouldn't know what to do.

I wondered if my internal fears of being away from home came from my experiences of seeing my Mother in court-appointed visits as a child. I was aware that I couldn't go out of the area with her because it was dangerous, so when young Hannah presented herself again in the form of CPTSD, it's something she brought with her.

But I told myself it was a good thing, so I decided I was going to go, and I would be okay about it.

It was the night before things that always got me. When it came to events that were out of the ordinary, out of routine, I went back to being someone who was crippled by anxiety and couldn't bear the thought of the unknown. I was nearly always sick.

I was so determined not to cancel because I'd booked the day off work to attend, and I really wanted to start building my life back up again. My therapist told me that enabling myself to miss out on events was enabling my anxiety to maintain control over my life, and so I needed to build on my experiences of all the things I have done that weren't so bad. If I go on the train and it goes okay and it's stored in my mind, the next time I go to get on a train will be more manageable. I needed to build up a bank of things to be stored in my brain to make them easier in the long run: eating out, social events, travelling, coping with busy environments. I had to desensitise the triggers.

I knew what I needed to do: make sure I eat dinner, make sure I drink enough water, get my clothes ready, read a book, meditate, go to sleep at a decent time. I thought that if I looked after myself as much as I could, I'd be able to deal with things better the next day – and I was right.

On the night before the event I slept okay and felt only a little shaky when I woke up in the morning. I focused on what I needed to do, just like I had the night before. I ate breakfast, brushed my teeth, washed, got dressed, put my make-up on, and straightened my hair. Step by step. I was alright.

When I got to the train station, I collected my pre-paid tickets and put my headphones in, forcing myself to think about how nice it will be to meet other bloggers. I stepped onto the train and sat on it for about forty seconds until it moved. I remember thinking to myself that if I really wanted to, I could still get off now, get into my car, head home and watch shit daytime television with a cup of tea. I can't lie about it – this scenario seemed a lot more appealing than the one that I was in. The train started moving and I focused on my phone, texting Charlie to tell him that I was on the train and would let him know when I arrived at London Bridge. He told me he was proud of me for taking a step forward.

Aware that my meditation app had a 'commute' practice, I felt quite comfortable that if I really became unsettled I would try this feature. I quite often find that knowing what my plan is should anxiety strike was highly beneficial. I always have a plan B.

Being unable to hear anything apart from my music put me into a little bubble on the train and I felt alright about just looking out of the window for most of the journey. But this was the calm before the storm. Train stations in London are busy and hectic and noisy and confusing, and I'm not someone who knows London well, like Charlie does. Some people know straight away which station they need, how far they need to walk, which stops are on a tube line, but

I just don't. Any time I've spent in London as an adult has been more about panic prevention than anything else.

When the train came to a stop, I stepped out into the fresh air and navigated my way to Heron Tower, using my phone to guide me there. I needed to be on the 39th floor of the building and I hated lifts, so I had made sure I'd get there early enough to be able to attempt to walk up that length.

As I walked into the building, I was greeted by a young man in a smart suit who directed me towards the lift. I told him I'd like to use the stairs instead, but he said that the stairwell was closed. I either had to travel by glass lift to what is described as 'the highest outdoor dining terraces in Europe' or turn around and forget about the whole thing, which would be a shame. The thought of getting stuck in that lift made me feel dizzy. I don't like to feel trapped in – I always have to know a way out.

I looked into the lift as the doors opened and somebody stepped out and walked right past me, like it was nothing. I had two things to battle with: the height and the claustrophobia. Before I had a chance to change my mind, I forced myself into the lift. I watched the doors close in front of me and closed my eyes instantly. I didn't want to see the ground moving further and further away as I ascended in what I can only describe as a fast-moving, transparent box.

I felt silly: people do this all the time and it's nothing to them, but to me, it was really, really hard. I hate to be made to feel like there is no way out. That's my problem with planes and tubes and lifts: if I feel I absolutely need to get out right now, I can't. I have to wait until I'm allowed to. The control is taken away from me.

I had my eyes closed the entire way until I heard

that we had reached the floor I needed. I stumbled out of it, not able to look around me.

There were two ladies from the PR company waiting for us all to arrive – I was the first because of how much time I had given myself to climb the stairs. They offered me a cocktail but I declined and opted for a coke. I wanted to stay inside my own head, be in control.

We sat and talked whilst waiting for the rest of our party to arrive, and before long a reality TV star and a presenter-turned-star walked in. It was a well-known London venue but I hadn't thought I would be sharing it with anyone famous.

The table was laid beautifully, with handwritten place cards and brand giftbags for each of us. I was sat next to one of the famous people that had joined our group, and I spent the whole time talking to her about various bits and bobs: her career, her children, mental health. She took a selfie of us and told me that I was 'so adorable'.

I didn't eat much lunch because it was a sushi restaurant and I don't like sushi. When everybody had finished eating, I decided to step outside onto the terrace – I wanted to see the view that this restaurant was known for. I knew that I might not like the height but I knew that I'd kick myself if I got onto the train to go home without just having a peak. I walked outside and spotted a comfy seat next to a heater and decided that I would sit there for a few minutes – it looked nice and it felt calm.

The terrace itself was beautifully laid out, and there was a stunning red tree in the middle of it, covered in lights. I thought about how great it would look at night. I stood up from my seat, zipped up my jacket and stepped towards the edge of the building, my hands reaching for the railing before I got to it.

Everything stopped for a second as I took in the vast view of the skyline.

By the end of the blogger lunch I was pretty tired – keeping yourself sane enough for a whole day in London isn't easy and despite having a good day, I was ready to get on the train home when the time came. I didn't hesitate getting in the lift this time – I decided as soon as I got up to leave that there was no point in questioning it. I had to get back in the lift to get home and if I'd done it coming up, I could do it going down. I got in, aware that I couldn't squeeze my eyes shut so tight this time because I was sharing the lift with another lady. Instead, I decided to turn my body ever so slightly, my hand gripping the metal bar, and I looked behind me at the view. I watched as the lift travelled lower and lower, moving us closer to the ground second by second until we made it to the bottom and I had to get out.

Back out in the open, I made my way back to London Bridge station and I took in the views the whole way. I'd never paid much attention to the city before because I was so focused on just being alright, but somehow, today, I was able to be alright and look around me with appreciation. I even felt calm on that walk back to the train station. There was beauty everywhere that I'd never noticed before.

When I got onto the train home I sent a message to Charlie and I told him how much I liked London now. I told him about the views and the restaurant, the terrace and the red tree. He wondered what on Earth I'd done with the Hannah he knew, and told me he was proud of me. I remember sitting on the train as it left London Bridge and thinking that I really liked the city – I'd seen it in a new light today. I felt calm and grateful and happy. I bloody love London nowadays.

Oh, how things change.

TWENTY

I carried on writing on Little Thoughts and I really enjoyed it, and I couldn't believe that my tiny blog was actually reaching people. I remember telling my dad that I'd reached 400 Twitter followers and how happy he was – you can imagine his reaction when the 10,000 day came.

After just under a year of blogging, I managed to get myself an award nomination. A kind, anonymous follower had voted for me and suddenly I'd gone from writing in secret in my bedroom to getting dressed up for a Kensington award ceremony.

I hadn't eaten much that day because nausea had started to set in as the awards approached. The morning had been fine because I was at work, but when I left at midday it dawned on me that I was actually going to London this afternoon to be in a room with hundreds of other people.

We arrived in Kensington in the early evening and

parked the car in a multi-story about ten minutes from the venue. Charlie changed into his suit in the back of the car as he hadn't wanted to crease it on the way: he's always smart.

We made our way towards the venue which was hidden away behind a residential area. There was a red carpet and lamps lit with burning flames, although it wasn't too dark yet. We walked down the red carpet and I watched as the photographer took a snap whilst I told Charlie that my shoes were already hurting my feet and that walking back to the car would be fun later. It was a beautiful venue and I appreciated the award nomination with immense gratitude, but there was a part of me, as always, that couldn't wait to get home.

We had about an hour before the awards started, in which time people socialised and ate. I sat opposite Charlie drinking rose lemonade in between stepping outside for a bit of air every so often. It was the end of June and it was warm, and with numerous bodies radiating heat it wasn't a pleasant experience for an anxious person. I knew I couldn't give in – I had to be there and I had to do this; writing honestly about mental health was the very reason I was sat here, so I couldn't let it be the reason I left.

There were pink lights reflecting off the walls and the venue was decorated beautifully, even if it was boiling hot. People grew quiet as the event started and the magazine's editor came on stage thanking us all for attending. It started quickly and before I knew it we were two awards in which meant my category was next. The editor introduced the lifestyle category and each nominee came up on screen and I could feel my heart starting to beat faster, harder as Little Thoughts appeared amongst the others. I looked at Charlie and I looked at a woman who was sitting a few people away from me on my table, who writes a fantastic and honest dating, relationships, and lifestyle blog that I read regularly and follow on every social media platform. All I could think was about how she was the one who deserved to win. I wasn't sad about it; she had more followers than I did, probably put in far more work than I did, and I thought her blog was far better than mine. And I've had a nice night in London with Charlie, had an opportunity to dress nicely and meet other bloggers and that, for me, was enough. I thought we might go home after this category.

Whilst I was thinking about all this my blog had been called out as the winner and I was suddenly 2017's 'Lifestyle Blogger of the Year', my eyes moving over to Charlie who looked so happy he could collapse. I remember thinking that maybe I hadn't heard right, but people were looking at me. People were looking at me and smiling and clapping and all I could think about was not falling over. I was at the back of the room – a classic anxiety tactic, I like to know that I can leave easily – so I had to walk all the way down the edge of the room to collect my award. That's a lot of time for potential falling over.

My hands were shaking as I took my award and had my photograph taken for the magazine. Still shaking, I was whisked off to have another photo taken against a beautiful flower wall – for social media this time – for the category sponsor. I didn't know whether to laugh or cry. Nothing would sink in. After the ceremony, people were coming over to me and saying well done, and my social media platforms were buzzing. We went up to the Winners' Lounge for me to collect my prizes: a whole load of products from the lifestyle category sponsor, which was a huge haircare brand. I could still only really focus on not falling over in front of everyone, and where the nearest exits or loos were.

The winners of the other categories were bloggers that I'd admired since I started, who had thousands and thousands of social media followers and even some who blogged as a full-time job. I couldn't believe that I was even in the same room as them, let alone that my name was next to theirs on a huge screen in front of everyone as a winner. I was informed that I would have my winner's interview for the magazine in the next couple of weeks and we headed back to the car, both of us virtually skipping on the way. We sent messages to our close friends and family sharing the news, and I responded to social media activity.

I felt like I meant something. I felt like the award represented much more than appreciation for a lifestyle blog, it was appreciation for mental health blogging. It was appreciation for people who write about their experiences and a reminder that people wanted to read it. People wanted to read what I had to say, and young Hannah finally had a voice.

TWENTY-ONE

It's strange to think of myself as somebody who seems to have 'come out the other side' of something. There were many times that I didn't think I'd have any chance of seeing life as I know it now. Life was waiting for me for all that time, patiently; I just couldn't see it. There has always been beauty in people, in nature, in moments, but I saw right through them. I could hear negative thoughts as if they were screaming through a foghorn, and see the worst of the world as if people's sins were scrawled across their skin. But love is quiet, and hope is quiet.

It's hard to look back on some periods of my life, but now I can look back at some of it with pride.

I think of the regular sight of a super berry smoothie. I think of standing on the terrace of one of London's highest buildings and the whizzy glass lift I took to get there. I think of Charlie guarding me on the tube with his arms spread out either side of him so that I wouldn't feel trapped on the train and both of us knowing how unreasonable and annoying it was for other passengers, but he wouldn't be moved for anything. I think of his endless efforts to guard me from gory or any potentially emotionally challenging television ads; his attempt to LA LA LA over anything that I wouldn't want to hear. I think of his face on the night I lost myself, heartbroken and desperate. I think of an undefeatable, urgent love that would hold me together until I found the strength from somewhere to keep myself upright – and even after that.

I always thought that love meant wild adventure. I guess sometimes it is. But even more so, the glaring definition of love, to me, is safety. Quiet safety.

I sometimes think about the way that a panic attack feels, how it will always be engrained within me. The feeling of crying for a third hour, the sight of my knotty, unwashed hair, the feeling of sheer, unadulterated panic: I don't think they're things I will forget too soon. I will probably always have CPTSD to some extent and it took me a long time to accept that I will never be the person I used to be. The symptom-free, confident girl I was in school, or when I met Charlie. I used to long for her – to be her again – but that won't ever happen and I used to find that really hard. I felt like I had been tarnished, taken over, and that the old me was gone forever when all I wanted was to be that person again. Looking back and remembering yourself as a broken version of who you are takes a long time to become easier, but I have only gratitude for the experiences I've had. I don't look back in anger anymore; I don't feel sad about it, I feel grateful. I feel grateful that my life experiences so far have made me kinder, more compassionate, more understanding. I feel grateful for the love and support that Charlie has given me and the strength this has given our relationship. It feels like my relationship can make it through anything now – and so can I. My mental illness made me question my purpose whilst providing it and encouraged me to be open and caring and to help others. There is so much in my life that I wouldn't know if it wasn't for the events leading up to now: my blog, my work, myself this book. The fact that I'm actually pretty bloody ballsy now.

Mental illness made me compassionate, grateful, deep. I took things for granted before it. Now I know the joy of being able to drink tea when I want to, to eat a meal, to drink a smoothie for enjoyment. I know the depths of my relationships; real, true gratitude; the importance of self-care; the power that lies within hope; how valuable life is. I learned that it's not about being happy all the time, but developing an understanding and appreciation for what helps me to get there and not putting pressure on myself to be my best self at all times. Sometimes I'm just trying to stay afloat, and that's okay. Staying afloat is enough.

I spent many days knowing that I would cry, that I would panic, that I would shake, and that I would probably throw up. I knew that my mind would talk to me, nag me, it would tell me things that I didn't want to hear. I knew that one small trigger could ruin me temporarily, that I'd be there again reliving experiences from clogged memories until my brain realised where I was again, that I am Hannah now, not Hannah then. I'd wake up in the morning and long for the night, but sometimes even sleep wasn't safe. There were times I'd experience flashbacks in my sleep, or nightmares, and I couldn't do anything about them but wait until I woke up. I wasn't safe awake, I wasn't safe asleep, and I often questioned if

I'd ever be safe again. It was times like this on which my brain would force me to reconsider. 'What about now? You still want to live this life?' No I didn't, but every single time I came to the very same thought: Charlie's face on that night at his house. It was his eyes as they pleaded with me without his lips moving. I'd never seen him scared until that day. There was a desperate look on his face that I hope I will never have to see again, but it was the face that kept me alive.

Now, I live the version of my life that I longed for whilst I struggled. A lot of my days now are spent anxiety-free, and I can go weeks without anything triggering me at all. Then, I may be at work, out with a friend, Charlie, or even be sitting at home with a cup of tea, and I can feel it coming. I can feel it coming like the flu, when your body starts to ache and you don't feel quite right and you know that when you wake up in the morning you will probably feel a bit rubbish and suddenly my body is consumed with fear, just like it had been when I experienced anxiety for the very first time. Just like young Hannah had felt. Sometimes it doesn't get that far, sometimes I spend some time borderline – I know it's there, bubbling away, and I can feel it in my body, but it doesn't escalate. It doesn't become panic. I've become quite good now at preventing panic but have come to accept that this is part of who I am. That younger version of me is part of who I am. EMDR isn't a cure for CPTSD and doesn't claim to be, for those memories will always be there. I will always have experienced what I've experienced, nothing can change that. I can only change how I perceive the experiences. Now, when I start to become anxious, I remind myself that it's just young Hannah needing reassurance. She's still living within me as a fragment of my brain: the piece damaged by trauma. I still look at young Hannah and hurt for her, but I guess I wouldn't be human if I didn't. You can only desensitise yourself so much, after all.

I don't know if I'll ever be wholly free from anxiety and I still occasionally feel like the girl who doesn't do things. The girl who can't. The girl that gets too scared and runs away home. But I'm not. I'm not the girl who can't, I'm the girl who can. The girl who will face anxiety whenever she feels able, and accepts when she doesn't. I can't be brave every day and that's not because of mental illness, it's simply because I'm human.

I think of her most days, my mother, but it doesn't make me so sad anymore. I might see a photo of myself, or notice something in the mirror, or sometimes I'll even say something and think I sound like her. I remember my therapist telling me that I was grieving for my mother, despite her still being alive. We associate grief with death, but it's not just death, it's loss. I was mourning a loss on and off for years. The thing is, my biology dictates that I would always look like her and behave like her. I'm always going to see her in the mirror occasionally or say something that makes me think of her.

But I'm okay with that because well, she's my mum. I may have lost her, but I've gained everything I need within myself.

www.littlethoughtsblog.com